THE ENGLISH ABBEY

Frontispiece

1 DOMINICAN NUNS IN QUIRE

*MS. Domitian A. XVII fol. 177 red.,
British Museum*

THE
ENGLISH ABBEY

ITS LIFE AND WORK IN
THE MIDDLE AGES

By

F. H. CROSSLEY
F.S.A.
Author of "English Church Monuments," etc.

With a Foreword by

THE RIGHT HON. W. ORMSBY-GORE
M.P., F.S.A.
First Commissioner of Works

*Illustrated by Photographs by the Author and
others, and by Drawings by*
BRIAN COOK

CLASSIC EDITIONS

This edition digitally re-mastered and
published by JM Classic Editions © 2007
Original text © FH Crossley 1935

ISBN 978-1-905217-87-8

All rights reserved. No part of this book subject
to copyright may be reproduced in any form or
by any means without prior permission in writing
from the publisher.

FOREWORD

By the Right Hon. W. ORMSBY-GORE, M.P., F.S.A.
First Commissioner of Works

Of England's medieval heritage we have left to us in the field of architecture the Cathedrals, the Parish Churches, the Castles and fortified Manor Houses, and what remains of the monasteries. Monasteries consisted not merely of churches but of conventual buildings as well, the homes and workshops of men and women devoted to the religious life amid the storm and stress of a rude and warlike society. Our heritage from the monasteries consists not only of superb works of art in stone designed and wrought for the monks by the best master masons of their time, but the works of the monks themselves. Of the latter the tangible remains are the illuminated manuscripts and choir books, and the monastic chronicles of our national history. Of the intangible there is the continuous legacy of Christian witness, the flame of learning and scholarship of which the monasteries were the chief centre, the tradition of hospitality and relief of the poor, and, as far as the Cistercians were concerned, the pioneer development of English agriculture as in wool production.

Heathen England was re-christianized by monks, by the Benedictines, who came first with St. Augustine of Canterbury and rose to great power and influence under Dunstan in Saxon times, and by the Celtic monks from Iona, who evangelized the Kingdom of Northumbria. Lindisfarne was the home of the first Abbot Bishops of the North, and from St. Hilda's Abbey of Whitby came Caedmon, our first English poet. The monasteries of

Jarrow and Wearmouth nurtured Bede, our first great historian.

Of pre-Norman monasteries the visible remains are few, those at Canterbury and Whitby being the most important, and these have only been made accessible as the result of quite recent excavation.

The Norman Conquest brought England into close touch with the Continent, where the eleventh and twelfth centuries witnessed a great outburst of monastic zeal and activity. The Conqueror himself founded the Abbeys of Battle and Selby, and transferred old Episcopal sees to new sites. Henry I introduced the Augustinian canons regular, and the new see of Carlisle was associated with an Augustinian priory. Under Stephen and Henry II came the great Order of the Cistercians, whose buildings are perhaps the greatest heritage of all. The monasteries were an outstanding feature of, and influence in, English life up to the time of the Black Death in 1349. From this scourge they never really recovered, and with a few notable exceptions, the story of the monasteries between the Black Death and the dissolution under Henry VIII is a story of gradual decay in popular influence and esteem.

As we read the story of the dissolution, the surprising fact is not so much the extent of the destruction but the extent of the survival of monastic remains in this country. Happily some of the finest monastic churches became, like Peterborough and Gloucester, new cathedrals. More, like Tewkesbury, Romsey, Selby, Bridlington, and Hexham became parish churches. But unhappily the majority were left to gradual ruin and decay or else were deliberately destroyed either partially or entirely. Nearly four centuries of neglect of these ruins, during which time nature even more than man has caused decay, have at long last been succeeded by a new effort to preserve more worthily the priceless remains. The Ancient Monuments Act of 1913 was a turning-point in the history of our monastic heritage. During the last twenty years a large proportion of our monastic ruins has come under the guardianship of H.M. Office of Works. The work of excavation, clearing away ivy, grouting remaining structures, and scientific conservation has entailed the public expenditure of many thousands of pounds. This campaign of preservation is but half completed to-day, but already Abbeys like Rievaulx, Byland, Tintern, Buildwas, and Netley have been transformed. Castle Acre Priory in Norfolk is an outstanding example of successful achievement. Work at Thetford Priory nearby has only just begun. The beautiful choir, transepts, and conventual buildings at Lanercost are now being taken in hand.

The ever-increasing number of visitors to the ancient monuments under the care of the Office of Works is but an indication of the reawakened interest of the public in our monastic remains. Official guides with plans are published, or are in preparation, giving a history and description of each monument in the charge of the State. But a really up-to-date general survey of all our monastic remains, with good illustrations, has long been needed. This gap is now well filled by Mr. Crossley's able and attractive volume. It will serve to bring home to many the vast extent and variety of monastic remains in England.

W. ORMSBY-GORE

November 1935

CONTENTS

FOREWORD. *By* The Right Hon. W. ORMSBY-GORE, M.P., F.S.A. v

PREFACE ix

ACKNOWLEDGMENT x

LIST OF THE PRINCIPAL REMAINS OF ABBEYS ARRANGED UNDER COUNTIES . . . xi

   I. INTRODUCTION: THE ORIGINS OF MONASTERIES—THE ORDERS 1

  II. THE CONVENT 10
      The Various Officers—Abbot—Prior—Sub-Prior—Precentor and Succentor—Sacrist and his Officials—Cellarer—Sub-cellarer—Kitchener—Fraterer—Chamberlain—Master of the Farmery—Hosteller—Almoner—Bailiff and other Officers—Monks and Canons Novices and their Master—Conversi—or Lay-brethren—Hired Servants—Other Inhabitants

 III. THE MONASTERY 37
      The Church—The Claustral Buildings

 IV. THE DAILY LIFE 56
      The Services—Life in the Cloister—The Processions

  V. ADMINISTRATION 65
      Management and Mismanagement—Spiritualities—Temporalities—Expenditure—Levies and Taxes—Pestilence and War

 VI. BUILDING 79
      The Layout—Building an Abbey—Canterbury—Westminster—Vale Royal—Transport—Accounts and Wages—Water Supplies—Drainage—Architects and Workmen

VII. SOCIAL REACTIONS 91
      Literature and the Arts—Hospitality and Almsgiving—Landlords and Landworkers—The Statute of Mortmain—Town Monasteries—Monastic Relations—Relations with Lords and Nobles—The Suppression

EPILOGUE & LIST OF BOOKS 106

MAP 108

INDEX 110

PREFACE

THE motor-car has revolutionised the face of the country and placed its treasures within reach. Among other benefits conferred it has fostered a growing interest in our historic places and ruins.

If their fascination is to be properly appreciated and understood some form of help is needed; hence this little book on the English Abbey, wherein an attempt has been made to visualise the former life which took place within the now desolate walls, and to show the nature of the ideals which governed the monastic outlook and work.

The volume is largely a compilation in handy form, from existing authorities, classified under subjects, for the general reader. Many of the records consulted are difficult of access, and by condensing and co-ordinating their contents it is hoped that interest may be aroused in the study of one of the most important institutions of the Middle Ages.

Without describing any particular abbey, sufficient details are given to enable a visitor to reconstruct the order of the various buildings connected with a monastery and to understand their use. Architectural categories have been avoided, the copious illustrations provided by a prodigal publisher taking their place.

I should like to express my indebtedness to the Right Honourable W. Ormsby-Gore, M.P., F.S.A., for his kindness in contributing the Foreword, written at a time of stress, and to Mr. Philip H. Lawson, F.S.A., F.R.I.B.A., for much valuable help in compiling of the text, and to the latter and Canon Charles Soulby for assistance in correcting the proofs. The provenance of the illustrations is fully acknowledged in the accompanying note.

FRED H. CROSSLEY

CHESTER
Autumn 1935

ACKNOWLEDGMENT

The publishers must thank the proprietors of *The Builder* for their kindness in permitting us to reproduce the plans of Durham and Fountains Abbeys. The former is drawn by C. Clement Hodges, F.S.A., for their Folio of English Cathedrals, the latter from J. Arthur Reeve's plan. The plans of Watton Priory and Mount Grace Priory have been adapted in line from the large coloured surveys made by the late Sir W. H. St. John Hope and Sir Harold Brakspear, published respectively in the *Royal Archaeological Society Journal* and by the Yorkshire Archaeological Society.

The publishers must acknowledge their obligation to the photographers whose work is reproduced in these pages, namely Messrs. Aerofilms, Ltd., for figs. 2, 138; Messrs. Carthew & Kinnaird, for fig. 17; the late Mr. B. C. Clayton, for figs. 4, 7, 11, 18, 19, 20, 31, 44, 45, 46, 48, 49, 51, 53, 55, 57, 63, 68, 90, 92, 98, 102, 103, 104, 106, 107, 112, 113, 119, 120, 124, 127, 129, 132, 137; Mr. J. Dixon-Scott, for figs. 3, 9, 10, 15, 25, 59, 60, 67, 71; Mr. Herbert Felton, F.R.P.S., for figs. 12, 133, 136; The Great Western Railway, for fig. 64; Mr. A. W. Haggis, for figs. 100, 101; His Majesty's Office of Works, for figs. 5, 123; Mr. R. Liddesdale Palmer, A.R.I.B.A., for fig. 128; The Rev. T. Romans, for figs. 115, 116; Mr. Walter Scott, for fig. 85; The Rev. F. Sumner, for fig. 58; Mr. Will F. Taylor, for figs. 6, 8, 16, 21, 22, 27, 29, 30, 32, 35, 36, 37, 61, 108, 109, 110, 130, 131, 134; Messrs. Valentine & Sons, Ltd., for fig. 24; Mr. Henry Walker, for fig. 135; figs. 13, 14, 23, 26, 33, 34, 38, 39, 40, 41, 42, 43, 47, 50, 52, 56, 62, 65, 66, 69, 70, 72, 73, 74, 75, 76, 77, 78, 79, 80, 81, 82, 83, 84, 86, 87, 88, 89, 91, 93, 94, 95, 96, 97, 99, 105, 111, 114, 117, 118, 121, 122, 125, 126 are from photographs by the author.

A LIST OF
THE MORE IMPORTANT REMAINS OF ABBEYS
ARRANGED UNDER COUNTIES

Denotes that the fabric is under the guardianship of H.M. Office of Works and is readily accessible to the public

B.	Benedictine Order	P. Premonstantensians	G. Gilbertine Order	N.	Nuns Church
A.	Augustine Order	Cl. Cluniac Order	A.P. Alien Priory	H.	Hospital
C.	Cistercian Order	Car. Carthusian Order	F. Friars Church		

BEDFORDSHIRE
    A.   Dunstable Priory   Nave of church in use

BERKSHIRE
    B.   Abingdon Abbey   Remains of monastic build-[ings
    B.   Reading Abbey   In ruins

CAMBRIDGESHIRE
    B.   Ely Cathedral   Remains of monastery

CHESHIRE [as chapel
    B.   Birkenhead Priory   In ruins, chapter-house used
    B.   Chester Cathedral   Splendid monastic buildings

CORNWALL
    A.   St. Germains Priory   Nave of church in use

CUMBERLAND
    C.   Calder Abbey   Extensive ruins
    A.   Carlisle Cathedral   Refectory and undercroft
    C.   Holme Cultram Abbey   Part of nave in use
    A.   Lanercost Priory (*ruined   Nave in use, quire and build-
            portions)   ings good
    B.   St. Bees Priory   Nave in use, quire intact

DEVON
    B.   Exeter, St. Nicholas Priory Part of buildings
    P.   Torre Abbey   Part of mansion and ruins

DORSET
    B.   Abbotsbury Abbey   Ruins, barn and chapel
    C.   Forde Abbey   Now used as private mansion
    B.   Milton Abbas Abbey   Quire and transepts complete
    B.   Sherborne Abbey   Church in use

DURHAM
    B.   Durham Cathedral   Monastic buildings
    B.   *Finchale Priory   In ruins

ESSEX
    A.   *Colchester Priory   In ruins   [mansion
    A.   St. Osyths Priory   Buildings used as a private
    A.   Waltham Priory   Nave of church in use; *gate-
                                                        house, etc.

GLOUCESTERSHIRE
    B.   Deerhurst Priory   Nave of church in use
    B.   Gloucester Cathedral   Monastic buildings

HAMPSHIRE [as church
    C.   Beaulieu Abbey   Ruined but refectory used
    A.   Christchurch Priory   Church in use
    C.   *Netley Abbey   Extensive ruins
    A.   Porchester Priory   Church in use

HAMPSHIRE—*continued.*
  B.N. Romsey Abbey   Church in use
  H.   St. Cross   Complete hospital
  B.   Winchester Cathedral   No monastic remains
HEREFORDSHIRE
  C.   Leominster   Nave in use
  C.   Dore Abbey   Quire and transepts in use
HERTFORDSHIRE
  B.   St. Albans Cathedral   No monastic buildings
KENT
  B.   Canterbury Cathedral   Monastic buildings
  B.   Dover Priory   Guest-house and fratery incorporated in modern school
  B.   Rochester Cathedral
  B.N. Sheppey Minster   Church in use
LANCASHIRE
  A.   Cartmel Priory   Church in use; gateway
  P.   Cockersand Abbey   Ruined except chapter-house
  C.   *Furness Abbey   Extensive remains
  B.   Upholland Priory   Quire in use as church
  C.   Whalley Abbey   Extensive ruins; gate-houses
LINCOLNSHIRE
  A.   Bourn Priory   Nave in use [used as church
  B.   Crowland Abbey   In ruins except north aisle;
  B.   Deeping St. James Priory Nave of church in use
  B.   Frieston Priory   Nave of church in use
  C.   Kirkstead Abbey   Chapel in use
  B.   Thorney Abbey   Nave in use
  A.   Thornton Priory   In ruins; fine gateway
LONDON
  F.   Austin Friars   Nave in use
  A.   St. Bartholomew's,   Quire in use
         Smithfield
  A.   Southwark Cathedral   New nave
  B.   Westminster Abbey   Monastic buildings
MONMOUTH
  B.   Chepstow Abbey   Nave in use   [an hotel
  A.   Llanthony Priory   Extensive ruins; west end
  C.   *Tintern Abbey   Extensive ruins
  B.   Usk Priory   Nave in use
NORFOLK
  B.   *Binham Priory   Nave in use
  Cl.   *Castle Acre   Extensive ruins
  B.   Norwich Cathedral   Monastic remains
  F.   ,,   Dominican church Used for secular purposes
  A.   Walsingham Priory   In ruins
  B.   Wymondham Abbey   Nave in use
NORTHAMPTONSHIRE   [nastic remains
  B.   Peterborough Cathedral ?Church in use, slight mo-

COUNTY LIST OF ABBEYS

NORTHUMBERLAND
- P. Blanchland Abbey — Nave and transept in use; gateway
- A. Brinkburn Priory — Church complete
- A. Hexham Priory — Church in use; new nave
- B. *Lindisfarne Priory — Extensive ruins
- B. *Tynemouth Priory — Extensive ruins

NOTTINGHAMSHIRE
- B. Blyth Abbey — Nave in use
- A. Newstead Priory — Now a private mansion
- A. Thurgarton Priory — Part of nave in use
- A. Worksop Priory — Nave in use; gateway

OXFORDSHIRE
- A. Dorchester Priory — Church in use
- H. Ewelme Hospital — Complete and in use
- A. Oxford Cathedral — Cloisters and chapter-house

SHROPSHIRE
- C. *Buildwas Abbey — Extensive ruins
- A. *Haughmond Priory — Extensive ruins
- A. Lilleshall Priory — Extensive remains
- Cl. Much Wenlock Priory — Splendid remains
- B. Shrewsbury Abbey — Nave in use

SOMERSET
- B. Bath Abbey — Church in use
- C. Cleeve Abbey — Fine ruins
- B. Glastonbury Abbey — In ruins
- B. *Muchelney Abbey — In ruins

STAFFORDSHIRE
- C. Croxden Abbey — In ruins
- B. Tutbury Priory — Nave in use

SUFFOLK
- B. Bury St. Edmunds — In ruins; fine gateways

SURREY
- C. Waverley Abbey — In ruins

SUSSEX
- A.P. Arundel Priory — Church in use; quire private
- B. Battle Abbey — Remains used as a school; fine gateway
- P. Bayham Priory — Extensive remains
- B. Boxgrove Priory — Quire in use
- H. Chichester St. Mary — Hospital in use
- A.P. New Shoreham — Quire in use

WARWICKSHIRE
- A. Maxstoke Priory — Tower and gateway
- C. Merevale Abbey — Chapel used as church

WESTMORLAND
- P. Shap Abbey — In ruins; tower left

WILTSHIRE

A.P.	Edington	Church in use
A.N.	Lacock Priory	In use as private mansion
B.	Malmesbury Abbey	Nave in use

WORCESTERSHIRE

B.	Evesham Abbey	In ruins; tower left
B.	Malvern Priory	Church in use; gateway
B.	Little Malvern	Part of church in use
B.	Pershore Abbey	Quire of church in use
B.	Worcester Cathedral	Monastic buildings

YORKSHIRE

A.	Bolton Priory	Nave in use; quire in ruin
A.	Bridlington Priory	Nave in use; gateway
C.	*Byland Abbey	In ruins
P.	Coverham Abbey	In ruins
P.	*Easby Abbey	Extensive ruins
P.	*Egglestone Abbey	In ruins
C.	Fountains Abbey	Splendid ruins
A.	*Guisborough Priory	In ruins
C.	Jervaulx Abbey	Extensive remains
A.	*Kirkham Priory	Ruined; gateway
C.	Kirkstall Abbey	Splendid ruins
B.	Lastingham	Crypt
G.	Malton Priory	Nave in use
B.	*Monk Bretton Abbey	In ruins
Car.	Mount Grace	In ruins, but interesting
B.N.	Nun Monkton	Nave in use
F.	Richmond Friary	Tower left
C.	*Rievaulx Abbey	Fine ruins
C.	*Roche Abbey	Transepts left
C.	Sawley Abbey	Considerable remains
B.	Selby Abbey	Church in use
C.N.	Swine Priory	Quire of church in use
C.	Watton Priory	Site excavated; Prior's lodging inhabited
B.	*Whitby Abbey	Considerable ruins
B.	York, St. Mary's Abbey	Interesting ruin
B.	York, Holy Trinity Priory	Nave in use

WALES

C.	Valle Crucis Abbey, Denbighshire	Considerable ruins
C.	*Basingwerk Abbey, Flintshire	Ruined
C.	Margam Abbey, Glamorganshire	Nave in use
C.	Neath Abbey, Glamorganshire	In ruins
B.	Ewenny Priory, Glamorganshire	Church in use

2 FOUNTAINS ABBEY, YORKSHIRE (*Cistercian*): Air View from the North-west

3 TINTERN ABBEY, MONMOUTHSHIRE (*Cistercian, 14th Century*), FROM THE NORTH-WEST

THE ENGLISH ABBEY

CHAPTER I

INTRODUCTION

MONASTICISM is not a subject easy of approach. The dust of battle has befogged it, and the various causes of bias for and against have made it difficult either to appraise its merits or to judge calmly its defects. It seems to stir up latent prejudices or enthusiasms, and it becomes almost impossible to take a disinterested view of its course and influence on the life of its times.

Its advent was caused by the manifold needs of the age, the outstanding feature being the prevalent cruelty and savagery, and the necessity of finding a place where God could be worshipped with some degree of quietness and safety, a place of contemplation and serious work in a world of anarchy and selfishness. The monastic ideal of St. Benedict was not attained without a period of endeavour and experience gained in various forms of asceticism. First, in Africa, the hermit lived a solitary existence in a cave or tent, contemplating the mystery of God and the ways of men, and, given a prophetic utterance, gathered round him a few devout followers who hung upon his words. As Micklethwaite remarks, "Every creed definite enough to excite a real faith in its followers has produced its monks. The Jews and Pagans of antiquity had them, and there are now probably more Buddhist and Moslem monks in Asia than there were at any time Christian ones in Europe."

After the period of the solitary hermit, who left no trace behind him, the religious-minded gradually gathered themselves together into companies, often of both sexes having all things in common, following no saints' rule, but producing bishops and missioners who did a great work in the christianising of the countries of Western Europe. Many of their traditions came from Ireland and can be traced back to the ancient British Church. They re-christianised our own country and produced men of outstanding character, including St. Colomba, St. Chad, St. Cuthbert, and St. Patrick. The north of England was their stronghold, although they reached as far south as Glastonbury, all before the advent of St. Augustine and his missioners with their Italianate ideas and outlook. Monasteries for both sexes existed in many parts of the country, one of the best known at Whitby under the rule of a woman, St. Hilda. These various monasteries were individual in their government, and however strict they were when first founded, gradually became secularised with the passing of time. The hey-day of their existence was cut short by the invasions of the Danes, who burnt the monasteries and put the inmates to the sword.

It was not until the reign of King Alfred that the country became sufficiently settled for a revival of monastic zeal, when a better system was found in the rule of St. Benedict. His followers were bound by three vows; to poverty, against the deceits of the world, to chastity, against the lusts of the flesh, and to obedience, against the snares of the devil. The chief duty of his monks was to take part with their brethren in the recitation of the canonical hours and in the celebration of the daily masses and services, a portion of the day being set apart for meditation, while the rest of the time was devoted to labour. In England this reform is associated with the name of St. Dunstan, Archbishop of Canterbury, himself a monk. Even under the rule of St. Benedict the monasteries remained independent, and were not governed under a single head.

With the Norman invasion a general refounding and the establishment of many new houses took place. The rulers and occupants were of Norman origin, a policy followed until the close of the twelfth century. With the first crusade came a wave of monastic enthusiasm, abbeys springing up all over Western Europe, and they were filled with men from all classes of society more quickly than they could be built. During this revival the stricter the rule the more it was sought and admired. The Benedictine Order not being sufficiently austere, a new order of reformed Benedictines was founded, sponsored by Abbot Odo of Cluny, all the houses being dependent upon the mother-house. This idea, excellent in itself, led to the impoverishment of the dependent abbeys, their funds being used for the aggrandisement of Cluny. When the donors found that the endowments given by them to their new foundations were being sequestrated they became disheartened, and the popularity of the Order waned. Although the Cluniac Order was in itself a return to the earlier simplicity

4 LLANTHONY PRIORY, MONMOUTHSHIRE (*Augustinian*), FROM THE NORTH

5 RIEVAULX ABBEY, YORKSHIRE (*Cistercian*), FROM THE SOUTH-EAST

of the rule, it rapidly grew into a great political and territorial power, losing its religious fervour. The buildings of the Order were more ornate than those of the older Benedictines, and the cloisters were ornamented with rich and curious carvings.

Towards the end of the eleventh century certain monks broke away from the abbey of Molesme in Burgundy to follow a stricter rule. They found a fitting place in a wild wood at Citeaux and there built themselves a wooden monastery where other monks like-minded joined them. For a time the hardness of the rule frightened away recruits, and the settlement was threatened with extinction. Stephen Harding, an Englishman from Sherborne in Dorset, one of the original members, became the abbot and the real founder of the new Order. Before he ruled, Citeaux was the poorest of all monasteries; when he died, it had become the head of an organisation which in a few years spread beyond the confines of Christendom and became the most powerful of all monastic Orders. It was puritanical in outlook and one of its inmates, the famous St. Bernard, thundered his denunciations against the luxury and temporalities of other monasteries, to which the Cistercians were a standing rebuke. In his *Apologia*, written about 1124, he says, "I will not speak of the immense height of their churches, of their immoderate length, of their superfluous breadth, costly polishing, and strange designs, which while they attract the eyes of the worshipper, hinder the soul's devotion. However let that pass; we suppose it is done, as we are told, for the glory of God. But as a monk, I say, Tell me, O ye professors of poverty, what does gold do in a holy place? for amongst us, who have gone out from amongst the people, who have forsaken whatever things are fair and costly for Christ's sake; who have regarded all things beautiful to the eye, soft to the ear, agreeable to the smell, sweet to the taste, pleasant to the touch, all things which can gratify the body, as dross and dung that we might gain Christ, of whom among us, I ask, can devotion be excited by such means? So carefully is the money laid out, that it returns multiplied many times. It is spent that it may be increased. By the sight of wonderful and costly vanities men are prompted to give rather than pray. What do you suppose is the object of all this? The repentance of the contrite, or the admiration of the gazers? Oh! vanity of Vanities! but more vain than foolish. What has all this to do with monks, with professors of poverty,

4 THE ENGLISH ABBEY

with men of spiritual minds? In the cloisters, what is the meaning of those ridiculous monsters, of that deformed beauty, that beautiful deformity, before the eyes of the brethren when reading? In fact such an endless variety of forms appears everywhere, that it is more pleasant to read in the stonework than in books, and to spend the day admiring these oddities than in meditating on the law of God. Good God! if we are not ashamed of these absurdities, why do we not grieve at the cost of them?"

Cistercian regulations prohibited anything savouring of pride or superfluity. Crosses were to be made of painted wood, the single candlestick of iron, the censers of copper. Silk was forbidden, and also gold and silver, except for the chalice. The first buildings of the Order were of the utmost simplicity, destitute of any adornment. The formation of an ascetic

Cistercian regulations prohibited anything savouring of pride or superfluity. Crosses were to be made of painted wood, the single candlestick of iron, the censers of copper. Silk was forbidden, and also gold and silver, except for the chalice. The first buildings of the Order were of the utmost simplicity, destitute of any adornment. The formation of an ascetic and ultra-strict Order was at once popular, and the founding of new houses spread with rapidity. When by 1152 the number had reached 330, the general chapter thought it wise to forbid any further increase. In spite of this, new houses continued to be founded, so that by the thirteenth century they exceeded six hundred. Those of the order in England numbered seventy-five. As an instance of Cistercian popularity, Rievaulx, founded in 1131, was able within six years to establish houses at Melrose and Warden, and continued with Dundrennan in 1142, Revesby in 1143 and Rufford in 1148. No ideal can stand the wear and tear of everyday life; it grows tarnished with constant usage, and dims with familiarity. Monotony is a great leveller, and monotony was the keystone of monastic life. The Cistercians like the earlier Orders suffered in time through a deterioration of ideals, the members gradually minimising their obligations. The cloister instead of being a refuge for humility became a pathway to ambition.

been shocked by the worldliness of the ecclesiastics of his time, was convinced that if you left the world, you must leave it altogether and shut yourself up within four walls secure from temptation. His rule was a return to the anchorite ideal, each monk living to himself in a separate cell, cooking and

6 BOLTON PRIORY, YORKSHIRE (*Augustinian*): the ruin of the 14th-Century Quire

7 FOUNTAINS ABBEY, YORKSHIRE (*Cistercian*), showing the Nine Altars Chapel at the East End and foundations of the Infirmary

8 MILTON ABBAS, DORSET (*Benedictine*): the 14th-Century Quire and Transepts

9 TEWKESBURY ABBEY, GLOUCESTERSHIRE (*Benedictine*), FROM THE SOUTH-EAST

eating alone, and rarely meeting his brethren except for certain services in the church, and then with his cowl drawn over his face. He led a life of isolation in the truest sense of the word, and devoted his life to prayer, meditation and digging in his little garden, and with the exception of the weekly walk taken with the brethren he never left his cloister. Such a life of austerity was forbidding, and the Order always remained small in numbers. They were the only monks who served no useful purpose to the country in which they lived; for good or ill they would have nothing to do with the outside world. They produced no characteristic works of architecture, literature, or benevolence, founded no schools, nor helped in the development of agriculture. They lived within themselves, devoted to saving their own souls. Peter, Abbot of Cluny, writing of them says, "Their dress is meaner and poorer than that of other monks, so short and scanty and so rough, that the very sight affrights one. They wear coarse hair-shirts next the skin; fast almost perpetually, eat only bean bread, whether sick or well never touch flesh; their constant occupation

ST. CHRISTOPHER, LIFE SIZE, AT NORTON PRIORY, CHESHIRE

is praying, reading and hard labour." The infirmary was absent from their buildings. If a monk was sick he was attended in his cell and when he died he was buried in the garb in which he lived, coffinless in the garth.

In addition to orders of regular monks, there were also orders of canons. Cathedrals and collegiate churches were served by secular canons, who were uncontrolled by a strict rule. The canons regular however lived together in communities under the rule of St. Augustine, being called Augustinians, and from their dress Black Canons. They were introduced into England about 1106, were fairly popular in the country, and were not as conservative in outlook as the monks. They had 218 houses and 170 remained at the suppression. The canons were never as wealthy as the Benedictines, their average income being quite moderate. Nevertheless they built some fine churches, Carlisle only reaching the dignity of cathedral rank. Although they lived in cloister according to rule, they had more freedom than the regular monks, and were allowed to serve in the appropriated churches placed under them, when it was found necessary. Unlike monks, who were generally laymen until the latter half of our period, the canons from the first were ordained and were governed by a prelate. They were independent, but held yearly chapters of the Order and were under the diocesan bishops. Guyot de Provens, a thirteenth-century monk, says of them that "The Augustine rule is more courteous than that of Benedict. Among them one is well shod, well clothed, and well fed. They go out when they like, mix with the world, and talk at table." We know much of this order owing to the preservation of the Observances for the Priory of Barnwell, Cambridge, an illuminating and instructive document, which is quoted in our later pages.

Another Order of canons regular was called the Premonstratensians, from their place of origin, or White Canons from their dress. They were founded by St. Norbert at Premontre and followed the rule of St. Augustine, but modelled their constitution on that of the Cistercian Order. Premontre remained the mother-house where the general chapters were held. In all about thirty houses were founded in England, which in 1512 were exempted from obedience to the mother-house and placed under Welbeck, the largest monastery of the Order in England. They chose secluded places and like the Cistercians colonised by sending out a nucleus from the existing abbeys.

10 SHERBORNE ABBEY, DORSET (*Benedictine*): the Nave

11 EVESHAM ABBEY, WORCESTERSHIRE (*Benedictine*): the Bell Tower

12 MALVERN PRIORY, WORCESTERSHIRE (*Benedictine*), FROM THE NORTH

INTRODUCTION

The Gilbertines were an English Order, founded by St. Gilbert, rector of Sempringham in Lincolnshire, its distinguishing feature being the revival of the double monastery, in which a society of regular canons ministered to the needs of regular women. St. Gilbert gave the rule of St. Augustine to the canons and that of St. Benedict to the nuns. "He culled from the statutes and customs of divers churches and monasteries as though he gathered the fairest flowers, and chose out those which he judged the more necessary and fitting for the weakness of men." There was to be a single master over all the houses, and no one should be admitted without his consent. During St. Gilbert's life, thirteen houses were founded, containing seven hundred canons and fifteen hundred sisters; there were twenty-six monasteries of the order at the suppression. The rule described the construction of these double monasteries, which is here given in brief. "In the priory church a partition wall divided the church throughout its entire length, the northern and larger half to be used for the nuns. The wall high enough to prevent the canons and nuns seeing each other, but not so high that the nuns could not hear the mass said at the canons' altar. On the north side of the church was the nuns' cloister, and it was to be better built and more beautiful and more honourable than those of the canons. The nuns were to be closely guarded and the window at which they spoke to their relations was to be the length of a finger and hardly as wide as a thumb, and was protected by an iron plate. In the frater of the men were two turn-table windows opening into the nuns' quarters, built so that they could not see each other, these were to be barely two feet high and wide. A high wall encircled the buildings. Three marks a year were taken from the pennies of the nuns to shut them in with moat and wall until they were secure. No expense was to be spared until the view and approach of all was shut out from them. The gate through which a four-wheeled cart could enter was to be protected within and without by bolts and very faithful guards." Nearly all Orders had houses for sisters or nuns, but in a few instances were they large or important. The finest church of nuns remaining is at Romsey, which was a house of the Benedictine Order, and the most extensive monastic buildings are at Lacock (90, 92) a house of Augustinian nuns.

There were two military Orders, the Knights Hospitallers and the Templars. The former were founded in 1092 with the building of a hospital at Jerusalem, their object being to provide assistance to pilgrims visiting the Holy Land and to protect them on their way. They followed the rule of St. Augustine and wore a black dress with a white cross upon it. They built their first house in England in 1100, and over fifty-three lesser houses were attached to it. They rose to great wealth and importance. Their head the Grand-prior was the first baron of England and had a seat in the House of Lords. Guyot de Provens says of them, "I have lived with them at Jerusalem, and have seen them proud and fierce. Besides, since by name and foundation they ought to be hospitable, why are they not so in reality? A monk in vain leads a hard life, fasts, labours, chants, and reads the scriptures, if he is not charitable; it is only an uninhabited house, where the spider weaves his webs." The Templars, who were founded about 1118, were supposed to protect the Holy Places and to secure roads to Palestine. They built their churches in circular form in imitation of the Holy Sepulchre at Jerusalem, several of which remain. They were rich and powerful, but being accused of great crimes were suppressed in 1309 and their property handed over to the Knights Hospitallers.

With the commencement of the thirteenth century a new type of religious appeared in the form of the preaching friar, whose purpose in life was to reach the masses, especially the poverty-stricken in the towns, and to minister to them both spiritually and physically. The monks and canons had made no attempt at missionary work, and the parochial clergy were inadequate for the needs of the time. The friars like the monks professed poverty; they were not allowed to possess property, but received their incomes from alms and oblations. The churches and dwellings were generally held for them in trust, and they possessed no appropriated churches or presentations of livings. The various Orders of friars came to England as follows: the Dominicans or Black Friars in 1221 the Franciscans or Grey Friars in 1224, the Carmelites or White Friars in 1240 and the Austin Friars a few years later. There were other orders, but the four enumerated were the principal ones. They were received with enthusiasm, to the annoyance of the regulars and secular priests, for they had the Pope's permission to preach and make collections in all parish churches. and were held in sufficient reverence by the people to make it a privilege for the nobles to be buried in their churches.

13 LANERCOST PRIORY, CUMBERLAND
(*Augustinian*): the 13th-Century West Front

14 WORKSOP PRIORY, NOTTINGHAMSHIRE
(*Augustinian*): the West Front

15 MALMESBURY ABBEY, WILTSHIRE (*Benedictine*): the Remains of the Nave from the South

They lived in convents, except those who had license to travel unattached, and their houses were under the supervision of their heads of their various orders. They encouraged learning and established themselves at both universities. Every house had its theological school, and they formed valuable libraries. The Franciscan house in London had a library which extended over the whole of an alley in the cloister. Many of their members and scholars rose to eminence—John Peckham, Archbishop of Canterbury 1279, was a Franciscan, and so were the scholars, Roger Bacon and Thomas Aquinas. But they were really missioners, work only realisable by social contact, the medieval counterpart of the Salvation Army of to-day. They laboured amidst the squalor, poverty and unwholesomeness of medieval towns, where disease and vice were rampant, and taught the ordinary man that he could be religious and save his soul without being immured from the world in a monastery. The friars were however the last efflorescence of the medieval time in the form of organised religious communities.

The country was turning away from monasticism, which had become a profession. The monks were rich and powerful; little by little the hardships of the rule had been softened till only the form remained. They had filled the needs of their time, keeping religion alive, and during unsettled and disorderly periods had materially helped in the development of the country, alike in learning, agriculture and the arts. As the land became more settled, people turned to other expressions of religion. The merchants grew wealthy, and the parish church became the object of enrichment and the founding of chantries a favourite form or religious devotion. New interests arose, the exploration of new lands, foreign trade, and the revival of learning. The establishment of colleges took the place of monasteries, and several years before the debacle many religious houses were suppressed and their property given to the new seats of learning.

CHAPTER II

THE CONVENT

THERE were many persons in responsible positions in a convent, the greater the monastery the larger the number of officers. Their status differed a little in the various Orders, but their work was practically the same in all. The head of a monastery was the abbot; but if the monastic church was the seat of a bishop, then the head of the convent was known as the prior. In the Cistercian Order the head was an abbot, but in the Augustinian Order he was generally known as the prelate or prior. All priories dependent on larger monasteries were called cells—even such a building as Tynemouth, which, though a large house, was dependent on St. Albans. The priors of all cells were elected by the mother-house.

The more important officers were known as Obedientiaries, and their departments were as a rule separately endowed and individual accounts kept. These embraced the precentor, the sacrist, the cellarer, the master of the farmery, the chamberlain, the almoner, the hosteller and sometimes the fraterer. Other obedientiaries were without endowments of their own. In the following pages an endeavour has been made to give an account of the work of each officer, and what should have been his character in office. These are described in the various observances and custumals which have survived. Because men are human the ideals therein set out were seldom attained, and the monastic chronicles are full of the mistakes and shortcomings of those placed in office. In a convent, where the selection was limited, men were sometimes given a position for which they were unfitted, the real character of the man not being disclosed until power was placed in his hands. The position of the head of the house was despotic, and he had to be a strong man to resist its wrongful use. The endowments of the obedientiaries were a further temptation, and many were led away from strictness and uprightness in the administration of the funds with which they were entrusted. The moral standard of the middle ages differed from our own. It was a time when might was right, and people were pertinacious in defending what they possessed, and were not particular as to the way in which it was done.

16 BUCKFAST ABBEY, DEVON: a Modern Reconstruction on Old Foundations

17 WHITBY ABBEY, YORKSHIRE (*Benedictine*): the 13th-Century Nave and Quire

18 BATH ABBEY, SOMERSET (*Benedictine*). The Roman Bath is in the Foreground

The world was a prey not only to enthusiasms but passions—a day of bright sun and deep shadow, devoid of half-lights. In judging these men and their actions it is necessary to remember these things.

THE ABBOT.—The head of the convent, whether prelate, abbot or prior, was the absolute ruler; he was the father, treated with the greatest reverence by his subordinates, and, with few exceptions, could appoint or depose any official under him. In the early days of the monastic ideal, he ate and slept with the brethren, and was the example to whom they looked for guidance in their own lives. There is a sketch of Ailred, Abbot of Rievaulx, at the close of the twelfth century, by his chronicler Walter Danial. "In his old age he had 740 men under him, and on great festivals the church was so packed with the brethren as to resemble a hive of bees. He was a mild disciplinarian, and it says much for his character that life was as smooth as it was. He was refined, courteous, gentle and firm almost to obstinacy. He was a man of pleasant and easy speech, with a memory stored with anecdotes. He was distinguished, industrious and physically frail. He had a distressing malady and lived and slept in a little room near the farmery, took hot baths, and as the end drew nigh crouched over a fire. He would talk with his monks, sometimes twenty together. He was friendly to the younger monks, and one of them became the staff of his old age."

This early patriarchal attitude of the abbot to his house grew into something quite different. He gradually withdrew from the convent to lodgings of his own, which became a separate establishment where he ate and slept and kept his own retainers; and he was often absent from the monastery for considerable periods on State or other affairs. He became very much the noble and great landowner, travelling about with a train of people, including sons of nobles sent to him for educational purposes. To such extremes did this go that Matthew Paris, describing William, Abbot of St. Albans, awards him a fulsome eulogy because he attended the services and meetings of the chapter and generally fulfilled his obligations when in residence.

A monk's nomination to the head of a house could be by election by his convent or appointment by the King or the Pope. If nomination was by the first method, it had to be confirmed by the latter. The abbot was expected to be well-educated and to have shown his capacity for management in subordinate positions before his elevation. "He should not only be skilful in ruling his own house and managing its estates to the best advantage, but in holding his own in defending by litigation the constant attempts made by outsiders to filch the prerogatives of overlordship and nomination belonging to the abbey. He was sometimes appointed by the Pope as a judge to determine cases, and required secular knowledge as well as being versed in legal intricacies." As Jocelin remarks of Abbot Sampson of Bury, "he was thoroughly imbued with the liberal arts and divinity as befitted a man of learning, a literate man, educated in the schools and a master of them, known and approved in his own province." As in all autocratic governments, if the head was capable and conscientious, and devoted to his community, it prospered, but often the reverse was the case. The prelate might be saintly but incapable; or he might be positively corrupt. In 1191–1213, Roger Norrys was forced upon the convent of Evesham by Archbishop Baldwin. Norrys had helped the archbishop against the monks of Canterbury, and Baldwin rewarded him in this way. His abbacy proved disastrous, "for he wasted the revenues, using them in extravagance, and in support of his relations and others, allowing the buildings to decay, so that finally the brethren had to live on bread and water and beg for a living."

A despot could override all rules. No measure of scheming and economy by the obedientiaries could counterbalance a thoroughly bad head. The reverse occurred at Dover in the treatment of Richard Wenchepe, prior 1268–1273. He was a quiet and inoffensive man who had done excellent work at Canterbury before his appointment to Dover. Following a dispute with the mother-house, involving a journey to Rome, he returned to find that the sub-prior had usurped his position and that the convent was in open mutiny. "Neglecting all rules and decency, the brethren locked the prior in his rooms for seven weeks, during which time the monks used his horses for rides to London and elsewhere, spending the revenues and scattering the property of the house." Eventually the prior escaped by night, trudging in the snow and mud eighteen miles to Canterbury in fear of molestation from the vagabonds infesting the roads.

THE PRIOR AND SUB-PRIOR.—If the abbot was the head of the house, the prior was the second in command; if the prior was head, then the sub-prior came second, taking first position in his absence. The prior was one of the officers whom the abbot could not depose without the consent of the convent. His position required tact and consideration, and it was essential for him to be in complete accord with his superior. His duties were to watch over the internal discipline and spiritual side of the convent. "He should go round the house during the day and correct those who were walking about or behaving in an unseemly manner. At night he should take a lantern and going round with his keys examine all the buildings and if he found any persons question them why they were there; he should see that everything was locked up, finally going through the dorter to assure himself that all was in order." The Observances state "that he should be remarkable for his holiness, his charity should be overflowing, his sympathy should be abundant. He must be careful to extirpate evil tendencies, be unwearied in his duties and tender to those in trouble, and he should set before all the example of our Lord. His it was to admonish the rebellious, encourage the timid, sustain the weak, be long-suffering with all, and a true physician of souls." The ideal prior is indeed a beautiful character, but the human one generally fell far short of it. In the early days the prior, like the abbot, ate and slept with the brethren, but gradually came to have an establishment of his own, where he ate and there received his guests. After a time his work was delegated to the second and third priors, and, like the abbot, he became a grandee in the outside world, its interests becoming foremost. Unfortunately the abbot and prior were not always in accord. At Westminster Walter de Wenlock and his prior Reginald de Haddham were estranged for many years, to the destruction of the peace of the convent and its discipline. Similarly, as we have seen, the sub-prior of Dover usurped the place of the head of the house to the great detriment of the convent.

THE PRECENTOR AND SUCCENTOR.—The precentor was one of the major officials of the convent. He was the chief singer, librarian and archivist, and organised the processions which formed an important feature of monastic ritual. The church services were under his management and were arranged by him. He picked out those who were to sing the lessons or responses, and "what he arranged to be sung had to be sung, and what he decided to be read had to be read." His place was on the right side of the quire, and that of his assistant, the succentor, on the left. He moved about the quire to regulate the singing and guard against mistakes. It was his duty to regulate the speed of the service; if the monks dragged, he must hasten them on. The Observances say: "Let the precentor or singer who sings surpassingly, comport himself in his office, which is a source of delight and pleasure to God, the angels and mankind, with reverence and modesty; let him sing with such sweetness and devotion that all the brethren may find in his behaviour a pattern for the religious life." The precentor went over the lessons and matins with the younger monks and pointed out to them mistakes in pronunciation and time. In some convents he was the instructor in music, training the novices and teaching the cloister-boys to read. "He was on no account to slap their heads or pull their hair, this privilege being the right of the master of the boys.

The precentor was the keeper of both the library and quire books, which he was to keep in repair and correct. The library was in the cloister in a recess, lined with wood to keep damp and insects from injuring the books. These were placed on shelves of varying height, and were enclosed by doors, the key being kept by him. He catalogued the volumes and kept a tally of those lent out. If application came from a neighbouring abbey or a noble family for the loan of a valuable book, permission was needed from the abbot, and its equivalent value required in exchange until it was returned. Many valuable books were the gift of the abbot, as at Croxden in 1303, when William of Evere, tenth abbot, enlarged the book-press and added many tomes. Transcriptions were made by the monks in the cloister, but no individual was supposed to write a volume for himself without permission. "If he showed pride about his work, he was to be punished by a course of bread and water." The precentor provided the parchment and pens, together with the ink, which was made from galls, gum, copperas and even beer. He kept the rolls of the abbey and also entered up the martyrology and the names of deceased members of the convent and their relatives. He prepared the mortuary roll, asking for prayers from other monasteries, and he was one of the three custodians of the convent seal and held one of the keys of the chest. The Succentor looked after the lists and saw that everyone was in his place, and was to help anyone who could not find his place in the book. At the night office, "if he saw any one of the brethren drowsy, he was to remind him to be more alert as watchmen keeping their vigil in the Lord's service."

19 ST. GERMAINS PRIORY, CORNWALL (*Augustinian*).
Only the Nave remains

20 RIEVAULX ABBEY, YORKSHIRE (*Cistercian*): the
13th-Century Transepts

21 CROWLAND ABBEY, LINCOLNSHIRE (*Benedictine*):
the West Front

THE SACRIST AND HIS OFFICIALS.—The responsibilities of the sacrist were many and important. He was responsible for the church and its contents; he and his subordinates were to sleep and take their meals there. He had the care of the ornaments of gold and silver, vestments and furnishings, to keep them safe from thieves, clean and in good repair. The shrine was in his charge, and the sub-sacrist was often delegated to watch it at night. At St. Edmundsbury in 1256 it was enacted that two persons should watch the body of St. Edmund, and two others the church treasure and the clock by day and night, for in 1198 the watchers fell asleep, and one of the

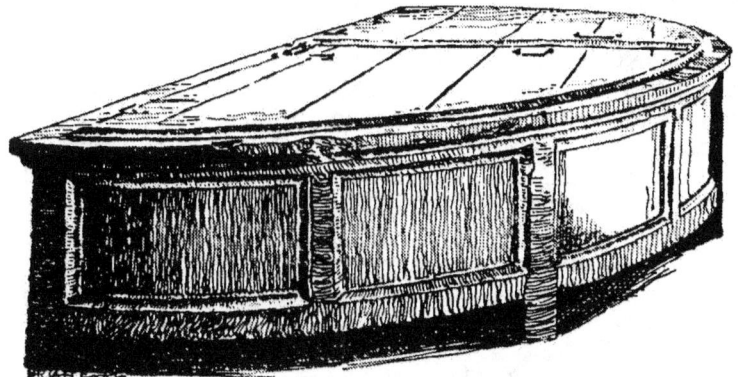

A COPE CHEST, GLOUCESTER

candles being insecurely fastened fell upon the carpets and the wooden platform before the shrine, setting the whole in a blaze, the church itself narrowly escaping. Among the duties which fell to the sacrist was the provision of live coals in iron dishes during the winter to warm the hands of those ministering at the altar. The sub-sacrist kept watch over the canonical hours, ringing the bells and regulating the clock. The sacrist provided lights for the church, fratery, abbot's hall, cellarium and guest-house. At Westminster the candles for the shrine and the royal tombs were a heavy item. For the tombs of Queen Eleanor, Richard II, Henry III, Henry V, and Henry VI over 1,434 pounds of wax were used. At the funeral of Henry V sixty torches each weighing $14\frac{1}{2}$ pounds were carried. The sacrist organised all the important funerals, the perquisites going into his funds; he also provided the obsequies of the brethren who died. Other matters included the providing of hay to be laid on the floors where there was no pavement, and the providing of organs and keeping them in repair.

The repair of the fabric came under his control. When he employed a plumber, glazier, mason or carpenter, he paid the wages; but the cellarer provided the food. The sacrist was also responsible for the greater undertakings. Alan of Walsingham, sacrist of Ely, on the fall of the central tower, was responsible for the arrangements for the erection of the great lantern. Sampson, the sub-sacrist of St. Edmundsbury in 1180, was master of the workmen in rebuilding the quire, and made preparations for the erection of the great tower, which was later under his charge. It must be understood that this does not imply that the sacrist was the architect or even made the plans; he was, however, responsible for financing their erection. The office required a man of no ordinary intelligence, but it did not mean that it always had one. If the abbot was old or incompetent, it was open to abuse. When Sampson became abbot of Bury, he deposed the sacrist, who had wasted the revenues and had pawned the altar furnishings during the old age of the former Abbot Hugh. "Furthermore, he commanded that the houses of the sacrist in the cemetery should be entirely plucked up by reason of the frequent wine-bibbings and certain other acts not to be named, which he with grief and indignation had witnessed while he was sub-sacrist."

THE CELLARER.—The cellarer was sometimes called the second father of the house, and he was certainly the Martha of his convent. His duties differed in different orders, but they were always important, and he often took second position to the head. In conjunction with the prelate, he managed the leases, buying and selling of lands, appointing of overseers, and was often away visiting the granges and properties of the convent. The cellarer and the prelate seem to have acted on their own responsibility in the most important matters; and provided they were in agreement, they could do as they pleased with the estates belonging to the house. "For in matters temporal the cellarer is as it were the prelate's right hand. After the abbot he has the first voice in his own office, and all his servants should obey him as though he spoke with the prelate's lips." He was responsible for the mills, the malt-house, brew-house and the tolls and carriage of goods. It was his duty to find out whether the men on the granges and their foremen were industrious, or received tips, or stole

22 GUISBOROUGH PRIORY, YORKSHIRE (*Augustinian*):
the 14th-Century Quire, East End

23 ST. MARY'S ABBEY, YORK (*Benedictine*): Remains of the 14th-Century Nave, Aisle, and Crossing

24 ROCHE ABBEY, YORKSHIRE (*Cistercian*): Remains of the Transepts. Late 12th Century

and sold the property of the house. He had the charge of everything concerning the food, drink and firing and of the granaries. The cellarer's good management meant prosperity; but a house was not always fortunate in this regard. At Bury, Abbot Sampson found that the cellarer was always in debt, and provided a clerk to help him with his accounts, to the indignation of the monks, who considered it an insult for a layman to be placed to watch the work of a regular. This, however, proved unavailing, so for a time he took over the office, saying, "I have often threatened to take the cellarership into my own hands on account of your defaults and improvidence. I put my own clerk in as a witness, but neither clerk nor monk dares to inform me the real cause of the debts. It is nevertheless said that excess of feasting in the prior's house by the assent of the prior and cellarer, superfluous expenses in the guest-house and the carelessness of the hosteller are the cause of this." In Abbot Ware's Customary he notes, "In the hearts of some servants there grows a weariness of divine work and worship and the cellarer had come to regard himself as more at liberty than was fitting." The temptations were considerable, and to be much abroad was more interesting than the routine of the house.

THE SUB-CELLARER.—The Observances say, "The sub-cellarer should be obliging, of a cheerful countenance, temperate in his answers, courteous to strangers, of polished manners, not to speak harshly and to know how to bear hard words from others, and, when he has no substance to distribute, to hand out a gentle reply; for a soft answer turneth away wrath." He was to be careful over the meals, and to see they were properly prepared and served with great promptitude, and also that no undesirable strangers came into his department. He might give the convent warm bread, but it must not be dirty, broken or burnt. At Westminster in 1402 there was an allowance of a quarter of wheat a day, and out of this John Longyng the baker made 40,880 loaves a year for the use of the convent. "When new barrels were filled with beer, they were not to be left without someone to watch them. In winter straw was to be placed round the barrels, and a fire lighted. In summer the windows were to be closed to prevent the heat reaching them." He was not to give new beer to the convent until the fourth day. The gardener was also under his charge, "he was wont to take three loaves daily for his two servants and their dog, and was to produce apples on St. James's day and certain other days, whether he had them in the garden or not."

THE KITCHENER.—The kitchener "had charge over all the things pertaining to the food to be cooked and served. He ought to be a truly religious man, just, upright, gentle, patient and trustworthy. He ought to know what food and how

BRONZE MORTAR FROM ST. MARY'S, YORK

much should be set before the convent, with special commons for the sick. He ought to have the help of a trustworthy man to buy the food according to the different seasons, to lay in stores of provisions with judgment, and to avoid waste and superfluity. He should keep an accurate account, a sum of the cost each week, so that at the end of the month he can render his account to the prelate." He was to see that the larderer was properly supplied with meat and fish, fowls and other birds, and to be careful about the keys and allow no one to have them without his leave, and not put too much trust in cooks and servants on account of the danger of temptation.

25 WALSINGHAM PRIORY, NORFOLK (*Augustinian*):
Remains of the East End

26 VALLE CRUCIS ABBEY, DENBIGHSHIRE (*Cistercian*)

27 CASTLE ACRE PRIORY, NORFOLK (*Cluniac*):
the West Front

The kitchen utensils were to be cleaned every day and never taken away. "He ought to know the number of the dishes, and the cook ought to keep what is left after dinner until the kitchener comes in, and render each day an account of the dishes handed to him. He must be careful that food is not served in vessels that are broken or dirty, especially on the underside, so as to stain the tablecloths. Further, he is to be careful that no food is set before the convent imperfectly cooked, or putrid or stale; and no excessive noise or clattering is to take place in the kitchen. The cooks should have the food ready in good time, so that at the sound of the bell after service the convent can go straight into the frater, lest the brethren may have chance to grumble." The food bought for the kitchen of the small house at Dover included "coddes, herring, whitynge, congers, hallybutt, muscelles, cockylles, mullettes, salt herrings, eeles, carpps, veal, sucking-pig, beef, pullets and vegetables." A plea of 1239 shows that the Abbot of Byland sued "Peter de Brus for 8,000 haddocks, the arrears of an annual rent of 1,000 haddocks which Peter owes and unjustly detains." In the account rolls of Bicester priory of the time of Henry VI is a curious item for twelve pounds of sparrow's eggs for thirteen pence.

THE FRATERER.—His duties were in the refectory. He laid the tablecloths and had them washed and repaired, and provided new ones when necessary. He poured the beer into jugs, which were to be washed inside and out once a week. He was also to produce after dinner two jugs of beer for the convent and its guests, one freshly drawn, but the other filled with the liquor left from the other jugs. He washed the cups and spoons every day and kept a tally of them. He also fetched the bread from the cellar, and was not to offer it if it had been gnawed by mice. When the bread was laid on the tables it was to be properly covered up. The fraterer provided the mats and rushes to strew the floor and the alleyways of the cloister near the frater door. He was to clean the frater thoroughly with besoms as often as this was required. In summer he threw flowers, mint and fennel into the air to make a sweet odour and he also provided fans. In winter he was to supply candles for the tables. If a brother sat by himself he had a candle, but if two or three sat together, they were only to have one candle between them.

The fraterer had charge of the lavatory, and was to remove any dirt or dregs lying in the bottom of it, so that the brethren might have clean water for washing their hands and faces. He was to keep sand and a whetstone always ready to clean and sharpen the knives, and to provide clean towels. The furniture of the frater was simple, but at Westminster it possessed valuable plate, the gifts of the brethren and the King. The frater at Durham was supplied with silver-plate, kept in an aumbry by the frater door. "Every monk had his mazer severally to himself that he did drink in, and they were all largely and finely edged with silver about them and double gilt with gold." It was a rule that anyone drinking should hold the cup with both hands as a sign of humility; during excavations in the Yorkshire Cistercian abbeys a few two-handled cups were found.

THE CHAMBERLAIN.—The chamberlain's office was domestic. With the exception of food, his department included all matters relating to the comfort and well-being of the convent. He and his assistant had the care of the dorter. He provided straw for the mattresses once a year, when the opportunity was taken for a thorough cleaning. He was to provide warm water for shaving and soap for washing the heads of the brethren, also baths, for which he had to buy the wood for heating the water. Baths were taken three or four times a year, and he bought sweet hay to spread round the tubs for the brethren to stand on. Hot water was also required for feet-washing on Saturdays, and a good fire had to be kept in the calefactory. The heads of the monks were shaved every three weeks. They sat silently in two rows in the cloister facing each other; the elder monks were treated first, and by the time the water was cool and the towels wet the turn of the novices came.

The chamberlain's principal work was the providing of clothes for the brethren. The tailory was under his charge and "he should provide tailors, trustworthy, sober, unassuming, secret, not talkative, nor drunken, or lying, as they were summoned into the interior privacy of the monastery, where they could hear and see the secrets of the brethren Such men should not be lightly engaged nor lightly discharged. The tailor should know exactly the shape and cut of the brethrens' woollen and linen garments. These should be neither sumptuous nor sordid." At Barnwell every canon had an outfit once a year, but at Westminster the brethren were served in rotation. He also looked after the repairs; in one of the Custumals any monk who wanted a garment

28 KIRKSTALL ABBEY AND THE RIVER AIRE: EVENING

From a Watercolour by Thomas Girtin

repaired placed it in the morning in one of the bays of the cloister, where it was collected and replaced when mended. He bought the cloth and skins required, either by interview or from the fairs. He was to find a laundress of good reputation and character to wash the linen, surplices, rochets, sheets, shirts and drawers; these were washed once a fortnight in summer and once in three weeks in winter. Great care was to be taken that no losses occurred and all articles were entered on tallies and returned in the same way. He looked after the boots and was supplied with pigs' fat from the kitchen three times a year to make grease to keep the leather supple. The sub-chamberlain was to supply the lamps for the dorter, to

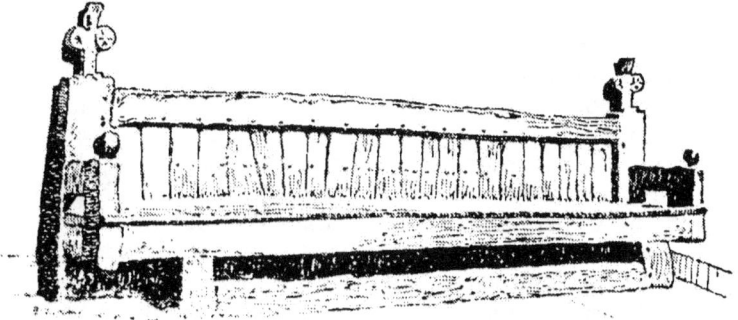

BENCH FOR INFIRM MONKS, WINCHESTER

light them and extinguish them. Illustrating the exact division of duties between the various officers, the sacrist supplied the dorter bell, but the cord came from the chamberlain. The sub-almoner provided the needles, but the sub-chamberlain the thread.

THE MASTER OF THE FARMERY.—The Observances state, "that he who has the care of the sick ought to be gentle, good-tempered, kind, compassionate to the sick and willing to gratify their needs with affectionate sympathy. He ought to have a servant who is to stay continually in the farmery and wait on the sick with diligence in all gentleness. He should get their food ready at the proper time, and note how they ought to be dieted. He must endure without complaint the foulness of sick persons, and when they die get their bodies ready for burial. The master ought to say mass daily, and if they cannot attend chapel, go to their bedsides, repeating words of consolation, but not disturb them when resting. He should take a kindly interest in each one and should provide a fire should the weather require it, and a lamp to burn all night. He ought to consult the physician and provide them with baths, draughts, electuaries and all other things conducive to a speedy convalescence."

Many diseases were treated with baths which were kept for the sick. In the larger monasteries there was a resident doctor and a physic garden where herbs were grown for the drug store. At Westminster there was an instance of a patient, Walter Twyring, who said he could not drink beer; this the master firmly declined to believe. The prior was called in, and in the end ten shillings worth of wine was bought for his use. Brother John, in entering up his accounts, adds the laconic remark, "so he says."

The farmery was also used for the infirm and the old monks, who were sometimes allowed a chamber to themselves. They were allowed books, which could be borrowed from the aumbry, but must be returned and locked up each night. If a brother was depressed he could go into the chapel and, when the doors were closed, someone could play music or sing to him to soothe his spirits. Conversation was allowed and, as Brakelond says, "they told each other the secrets in their hearts." Three kinds of sick persons are mentioned, "those who are in weak health from irksomeness of life in the cloister, long-continued silence, fatigue in the quire, extension of fasting and sleeplessness from overwork. Others suffer from overloading their stomach and drinking and sitting up late with guests; and if severely punished move about as though half dead. The cure for these ailments is not the farmery but change. The second are those who have attacks of tertian fever, intolerable toothaches, gout, affections of the brain, eyes, throat, spleen, liver, and pains in divers parts of the body. The third are struck with illness so sudden that they lose the strength of their limbs in an instant. These last two sorts go into the farmery." It was also used by those who were periodically bled, and they were allowed to spend three days there. This occurred at intervals of a month to seven weeks. The different Orders had different times for bleeding, and the Cistercians did not allow those who were bled into the farmery, but they slept in the dorter.

The refractory monks were also sent to the farmery, and at Durham there was a prison attached, called the lynghouse, which was ordered for such as had committed grave offences.

29 RIEVAULX ABBEY, YORKSHIRE (*Cistercian*) : looking across the 13th-Century Quire

30 GLASTONBURY ABBEY, SOMERSET (*Benedictine*), LOOKING WEST. The most sacred spot in England

The Durham Rites say, "That he should sit there for a whole year in chains without anyone seeing him but the master, who let down his meat through a trap-door by a cord, being a great distance from them." At Ely they had a place called "helle," which was no doubt for the same purpose. It was usual to send refractory monks to other houses for treatment. Abbot Gregory of Whalley addressed a letter to the Abbot of Kirkstall, "Since the visitors decree that the bearer of this letter, one of our monks and a priest, is under punishment for conspiracy, and since he has for a year and more humbly and devotedly undergone the penance therefor; and as we cannot consistently with the peace of the brethren and the discipline of the order keep him any longer in our house, we beg you that you would keep him thus sent to you, with the right amount of clothing, amongst your brethren, treating him and causing him to be treated by others in the proper manner until we have licence to recall him. Let him be the last of the priests in the church, nor let him celebrate. Every Friday in Advent and Lent under penance of bread and water let him receive discipline in the chapter. I promise to repay you with a similar attention." A letter from an exiled monk from St. Albans describes the cell at Tynemouth to which he had been sent: "Our house is confined to the top of a rock, surrounded by the sea on all sides but one. Day and night the waves break and roar, thick sea frets roll in, wrapping everything in gloom. Dim eyes, hoarse voices, sore throats are the consequences. Spring and summer never come here. The north wind is always blowing, and it brings with it cold and snow or storms of wind. No ring dove or nightingale is here, only grey birds whose screaming denotes a storm. See to it, brother, that you do not come to so comfortless a place."

THE HOSTELLER.—The monastery was the inn of the Middle Ages, with this difference, that the guests did not pay for their entertainment. Of this full advantage was taken, and the drain on the finances of the convent at times reached breaking-point, especially when the house stood near constant traffic, as at Dover and Birkenhead. The latter complained bitterly to Edward II over the ferry between Liverpool and Wirral, when people had to wait for days before they could cross; and the only habitation on the Wirral side was the priory. The house was so "often burdened with so many sojourners that it can no longer endure; the house has not sufficient for all the multitude of those passing and coming.

They asked leave to build houses at the ferry and sell food to the passengers for the safety of the people and the relief of this poor house." Writing at the beginning of the thirteenth century the monk Lucian wonders how the monks of Chester do not tire of their good humour. "They are joyful to the men of the county, business-like to travellers from afar. The seats about their table are worn by reason of the many meals given to strangers, such is their innate liberality. Here travellers to and from Ireland find rest, companionship and shelter while waiting for wind and tide." At Durham they had a noble guest-house, "the entertainment not being inferior to any place in England, both for goodness of their diet, the sweet and dainty furniture and generally all things necessary for travellers. In the hall was a great fire and the chambers belonging to it were most sweetly kept and richly furnished; the victuals came from the kitchen of the prior without stint."

The Barnwell Observances give what should be the character of the hosteller: "As it is proper for him to converse with guests of different sexes and condition, it becomes him to have not merely facility of expression but elegant manners and a respectable bringing up. If he have no substance to bestow, he may at any rate exhibit a cheerful countenance and agreeable conversation. By showing cheerful hospitality to guests, the reputation of the monastery is increased, friendships multiplied, animosities blunted, God is honoured, charity increased and a plenteous reward in heaven is promised." It was the duty of the hosteller to see that perfect cleanliness and propriety were found in his department, clean clothes, clean towels, cups without flaws, spoons of silver, mattresses and blankets, and sheets not merely clean but untorn, quilts of full width and length and of a pleasing colour to the eye; in winter candles and candlesticks, a fire that does not smoke; writing materials; the whole guest-house kept clear of spiders' webs and dirt, and strewn with rushes underfoot. "He should have a faithful servant, who is not to go to bed until the guests have retired. He should be up early when the guests leave, to see that they do not forget a sword or a knife, and that the property of the convent is not accidentally taken away." This last injunction was necessary, for at Dover the prior speaks feelingly of the loss sustained, from strangers, "who were such wasteful destroyers that it is impossible to keep things in order. Strange ambassadors had such noxious and hurtful followers, that they packed up the

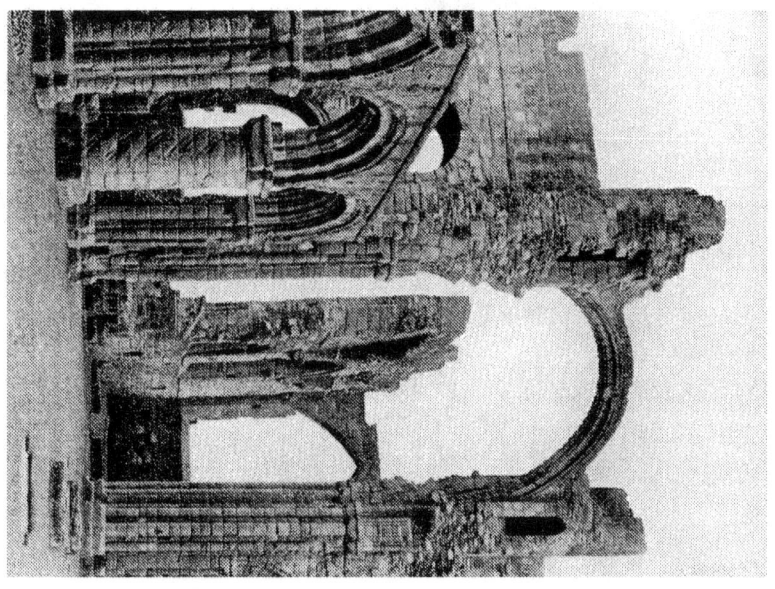

31 LINDISFARNE PRIORY, NORTHUMBERLAND (*Benedictine*): View of the Crossing, 12th Century

32 BYLAND ABBEY, YORKSHIRE (*Cistercian*): the 13th-Century West Front

33 CALDER ABBEY, CUMBERLAND (*Cistercian*):
the Nave Arcade

34 TEWKESBURY ABBEY, GLOUCESTERSHIRE (*Benedictine*):
the Eastern Range of Chapels

tablecloths, napkins, sheets and coverpanes and such things as they could lay hold of." Royalty lodged in monasteries, whenever it suited its convenience; Reading Abbey was built as an inn for the king on his progresses to and from Gloucester. Some kings were generous, but others, like King John, were not. He stayed at Bury for ten days with all his retinue and offered thirteen pence and a silk cloth, which he had commandeered from the sacrist and for which he forgot to pay. At St. Albans they had stabling for three hundred horses, and at Abingdon had a special endowment for providing new shoes for the horses of the guests. The cost of keeping open house was very heavy, especially when travellers had many retainers and stayed for several days. At Thetford in 1279 the house was crippled by the residence of its patron, the earl marshal's brother; he was costing the house more than the whole number of the monks put together. The difficulty of regulating the finances under such circumstances must have been more than serious.

THE ALMONER.—"Ought to be kind, compassionate and God-fearing. He ought to be discreet and careful in his apportionments, to endow with more copious largess, pilgrims, palmers, chaplains, beggars and lepers. Old men decrepit, lame and blind or who are confined to their beds, he ought frequently to visit and give them suitable relief. He should submit to the loud-voiced importunities of the poor with calmness and ought not to strike or hurt or even abuse or upbraid anyone, but answer them with patience and moderation." At Westminster he was carefully to inquire in person the whereabouts of sick people who were too poor to provide for their own needs. He must take two servants with him, and before he enters a house must inquire if there are women within. If so, the latter must first leave. He was not to attend to the sick folk of the other sex, but send what was necessary by one of his servants. A number of old or sick folk lived in the almonry. At Malvern they had twenty resident poor bedesmen, together with the singing boys and the school lads. At Westminster the lay-brothers also lived there.

The almoner's duties included finding the poor men whose feet the monks washed on Thursdays, and the supervision of the letter-carriers who brought rolls of deceased persons. He and his assistant were to guard the cloister from intruders, to sweep and keep it clean, also the chambers of the sick, and to strew them with fresh hay and straw. He collected the fragments from the meals for distribution to the poor, together with the discarded clothing of the convent. At Westminster before Christmas he bought seventy-five measures of russet cloth to be divided between twenty-five poor folk.

The children of the almonry and the song school were clothed and fed by the monastery. At Westminster in due course the sub-almoner took them to London to be apprenticed to masters of various trades. They wore russet-coloured fustian, lined with white cotton, bound with black velvet and tied with silken points. The convent kept a watchful eye upon them and visited them with gifts when sick. In the almoner's roll at Westminster for 1319 is an item of "thirteen shillings and eightpence to keep little Nigel at school for a whole year for the love of God." At Barnwell "the boys who lived on charity in the almonry were to be set to argue against each other and to be kept under the rod, so that they might learn better. On feast days, when not at school, they were to read and sing in church, learn to write on parchment, and repeat by heart their letters and explain the different meaning of words, instead of running about the streets, fighting and disputing. Otherwise the almoner should turn them out and substitute well-conducted scholars in their place." He had to keep an eye on the permanent chaplains who lived in the almonry, "that they do their duties and lead honourable lives. He should be aware of any improper actions on their part and admonish them in secret. If they were rebellious he should chastise them; and as he ought to honour and love the good, so he ought by no means to put up with the insolence of the bad."

The monastery usually provided some education outside its own departments. At Ely "the singing school was a pretty house, with two rooms in the occupation of Robert Claxton, the singing master. At the stair head over against the school door was another room with a parlour taken out of it for a place to play the vyall in. Robert Hynde, clerk and usher to the free school, held a little tenement next the singing school and another little room at the stairs' head with a kitchen vaulted beneath." At Durham the school for poor children was in the farmery chamber without the abbey gate. The schoolmaster was one of the monks, who lived over the farmery and said mass in its chapel.

THE BAILIFF AND OTHER OFFICERS.—At Westminster there was a monk-bailiff who was treasurer and keeper of accounts.

35 MALMESBURY ABBEY, WILTSHIRE (*Benedictine*):
the Norman South Porch

36 STRATA FLORIDA ABBEY, CARDIGANSHIRE (*Cistercian*):
the West Doorway

He visited the manors and held the customary courts there together with the steward. He was the legal official of the convent, having his own household and entertaining convent guests. The general treasurer made payments of all kinds in addition to ordinary accounts, including the students at Oxford, and an outing for the whole convent to Battersea by way of recreation once a year. He paid the Maundy distribution to the poor, liveries for the lay-officers and hired servants, contributions to the singing men, and for the shoeing and medicine for the horses.

The property of the Augustinian houses was cared for by a grainger and two receivers. "Whatever belonged to bread and beer, to seed and allowance, ought to come out of the granary; whatever belonged to money, by the hands of the receivers. Therefore neither the sub-cellarer nor the kitchener, nor the servants at wages, can conveniently discharge their duties, unless their departments are supplied by adequate and punctual disbursements of the grainger and the receivers. They should set down on tallies all the profits of the manors and write tallies of each, so that when the prelate chooses he may inspect the accounts."

The Gilbertines, a small community, had a faithful brother for a grainger, whose duty it was to see that all lands were sown with seed best suited to them. If he neglected this duty, he was allowed only one loaf of bread a day until the crops were reaped. He went round in the autumn with the threshers to thresh out all the grain required for the convent for a whole year, the rest being sold for the profit of the house. He kept tally of all the corn paid in tythe from appropriated churches. He was responsible for the cheese and butter, geese, chickens and bees, and that the house was supplied with all these commodities.

The lives of the bailiffs and graingers were not always easy. In the chronicles of Crowland concerning their church at Whaplode in 1481, it states that the parishioners were cutting down the abbot's trees in the churchyard. On hearing this he sent his bailiff, Alan Dawson, to forbid it. They replied, "What say, you monk? We shall that, and though the abbot himself were here continue to do so, and if he objected we should cut off his head." The bailiff, alarmed, ran for safety to the church, the woodcutters after him with their axes. The enraged populace rushed on him, tore his cloak to pieces, nearly strangled him and took away his purse. The vicar, who was hearing confessions, rescued him, locking him in the vestry for safety. There they compelled him to write to the abbot, demanding his consent, or else send two sacks, one for the bailiff's head, the other for his body. The bailiff spent the night in the vicarage, the insurgents, armed with "jakkes, salettes" and weapons, surrounding the house for fear of his escape, others for the same reason sat up till midnight in the steeple to watch. This was at the close of the fifteenth century, when the monks were regarded as exacting landlords and the reverence for the religious was on the wane.

THE MONKS AND THE CANONS.—In the earlier periods under strict rule, the life of the regulars was one of hardship. They were allowed no possessions; their clothes were provided for them, and when worn recalled and given away. They were not supposed to possess even a knife, a needle or a pen or writing tablets; they saw no money and were obedient in all things. They spent their time in innumerable services and study, living a dull existence in silence, shut away from the world and its excitement, for they lived on a low diet and suffered much from indigestion, a prey to habits which cut across the precepts of good health, and the constant and periodical bleedings were weakening. The average life of a monk was fifty-five years. The picture of a monk's life during an English winter is not to be envied, with no heating in the monastery, the dorter icily cold when he rose for the long night service, going half asleep in the dark to a freezing church, perhaps filled with a clinging fog, and being expected to sing and pray with fervour for an hour and a half. As Haines says, "The routine, the monotony, the utter weariness of it must have been such as we can scarcely conceive." One can understand the Dover and many other unseemly incidents recorded, for human nature must often have been on the point of open rebellion. It is said the monks loved tittle-tattle and hearing of news from the outside world, and so they might under the circumstances.

The Visitation of Archbishop Winchelsay to Dover in 1299 is instructive as to the conditions of a monastery at that time. Amongst other injunctions he says, "No monk must absent himself from the services unless sick. There shall be no excess of food or drink, that even the most captious can criticise. The strict rule of St. Benedict is to be kept. As the convent is burdened with debt, let the brethren cut off all superfluities of food and drink and think only of the necessities of the poor. When not at services they must remain in cloister, and not stand about gossiping with new arrivals, asking for news and idling. As food is provided by the cellarer, so clothes are to be provided by the chamberlain, and for the future monks are not to be given money in lieu of garments or to expend it at their own discretion, lest it give rise to a notion of ownership or some other illegitimate desire. No funds earmarked for almsgiving should be used for paying the convent's debts. Since the dwellers in the cloister require quiet for prayer and study, all doors are to be closed and no layman permitted to cross it. No monk, official or other may lend or borrow money without permission of the prior, for the taint of ownership cannot but attach to a violation of this rule." A visitation of Archbishop Wareham in 1511 shows that in his time the monks received pocket money or stipends. One complaint against a house was that owing to the pension being paid in kind no monk would enter it. Possession of money became general, and even as early as 1330 in one house each monk owned silver plate to the value of fifteen to twenty pounds. In another instance one pound, six shillings and eightpence was paid to each monk as pocket money.

THE NOVICES AND THEIR MASTER.—The master of the novices was a senior monk, responsible and earnest. It was his duty to watch, teach and clothe them, "and if any of them were apt to learning and did apply his books, and had a pregnant wit withall, then the master did let the prior have intelligence and he was sent to Oxford to school and there did learn to study Divinity, and the residue of the novices were kept at their books till they could understand their service and the scriptures." At Durham they were taught in the west side of the cloister, "where there was a fair great stall of wainscot where the novices did sit and learn, and the master had a pretty stall adjoining on the south side of the treasure-house door, and there he sat and taught the novices both forenoon and afternoon, and no persons were allowed to trouble them, and a porter was appointed to keep the cloister door for that purpose." It was the custom for the larger monasteries to have six novices, in the lesser houses three, as at Dover where Archbishop Wareham "found that there were three novices not instructed in grammar, and that there was no instructor except the sub-prior, and he read to them the gospel twice a week and nothing else."

Novices were supposed to be at least seventeen years of age

on their admission, and boys and unsuitable persons might not be received, nor illegitimates without special permission. Until he became professed he was treated as a schoolboy and kept under severe discipline. The Barnwell Observances say: "In selecting novices the brethren should be careful not to choose those whose election they may afterwards repent. They should ask as to their country, parentage, knowledge, behaviour, voice and power of singing, capacity of writing, and of executing any mechanical art; next as to their bodily stature, whether they possess everything they ought to possess, whether they have incurred obligations elsewhere, or consort with any woman; whether they are in debt, if they have any secret malady, whether they are good-tempered, sociable, trustworthy and of good character, and finally if they are likely to be of use to the monastery. If all these things prove satisfactory, the novice ought to be received by the prelate in full chapter; he ought to point out the strictness of the Order, perpetual chastity, poverty and obedience. In the next place he should make it plain he must render obedience from the heart. If he assents he will admit him by the kiss of brotherhood."

Before he was clothed he had to confess his whole life to the prelate. He was then shaved and reclothed in the correct garments. He was again asked before the whole chapter if he was prepared. The prelate then granted him a year's probation, and assigned him to a master who was to teach him the details of dress and behaviour and all the observances of the rule, how to live not only during the first year, but during his whole habitation. For a time the master stayed with him day and night watching and instructing him in every little detail. At the year's end, should he be amiable, sober, chaste, devoted to God, proper for a religious life and well disposed, he was to be asked if he could endure with a good heart nocturnal vigils, a dull life in cloister, continual services in quire, prolonged silence, the strictness of the Order, and the different characters of the brethren. If he replied in the affirmative, he was professed; if not, he could depart in his secular habit back into the world.

In 1141 at the Cistercian convent of Rievaulx, Ailred, afterwards abbot, was master of the novices. Whilst teaching them he wrote a book in the form of a dialogue, from which I extract the following, from a translation by Professor Powick: "The newcomer had been perplexed by the contrast

37 FOUNTAINS ABBEY, YORKSHIRE (*Cistercian*):
the West Doorway

38 NORTON PRIORY, CHESHIRE
(*Augustinian*)

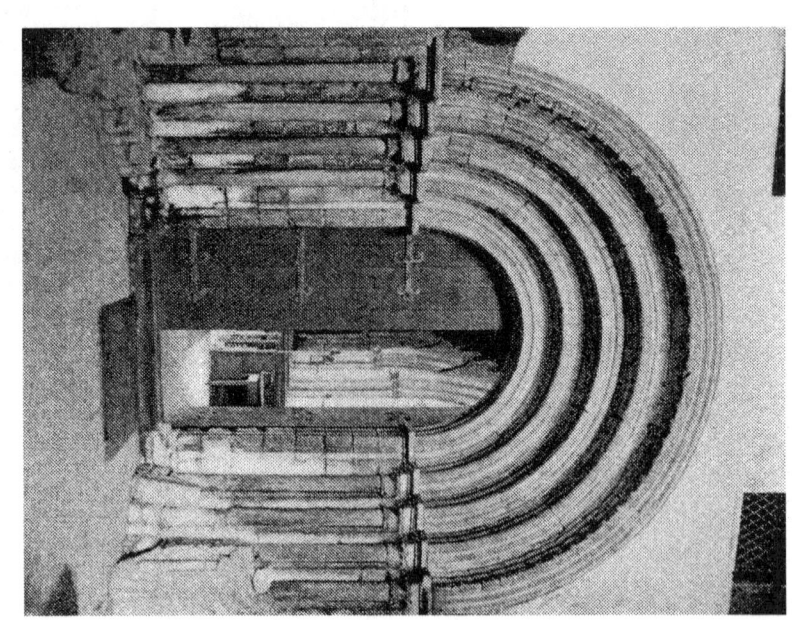

39 HOLME CULTRAM, CUMBERLAND
(*Cistercian*): the West Doorway

between the spiritual rapture of the past and the aridity of the present. Ailred led him to analyse his early experiences. They had been delightful but passed as quickly as they came. He found equal pleasure in devout tears and in worldly jests. Now life was different; scanty food, rough dress, water from the well, a hard pallet. The bell rang just when sleep was sweetest. He had to toil and sweat for his daily bread, his conversation with his fellows was confined to a few necessary words with three people. He gladly agreed that this was only one side. Discipline meant peace; no wrangling or complaints of injustice, no law-suits, no respect to persons in high places, no favouritism in daily tasks. He was now a member of a community united by a common interest. Then Ailred brought him face to face with the issue. The conclusion was drawn: to love is one thing, to love with full surrender a harder thing. Love without service is like the emotion of the playgoers who weep at the sight of sufferings, which in the street they would pass unmoved. The novice hung his head. He remembered how he who had been so lightly moved to tears for his love of Christ, had been wont to cry with equal facility over the story of Arthur."

THE CONVERSI OR LAY-BRETHREN.—The conversi were not admitted to the habit, unless they were instructed in some craft which was useful to the monastery, "for as regular canons ought to be occupied day and night in things spiritual; so lay-brethren ought to labour for the profit of the church in things corporal; for in a monastery no one ought to eat his bread unless he work for it. At the outset the prelate ought to designate some God-fearing canon who is diligently to teach the lay-brother the duties of his station, so that if possible he may learn to say the 51st psalm, the 150th and the confession." In the Cistercian statutes of 1256 it is enjoined that no conversus is to have a book, or learn anything save the Paternoster, the Creed, the Miserere and the rest which is decreed they ought to say, and this not by letter but by heart. There were a few conversi in nearly all Orders, but in the Cistercian Order in the early years they formed the greater number in the monastic house. At Rievaulx during Ailred's time there were 140 monks and 600 conversi. At Waverley in 1187, fifty-nine years after its foundation, there were 70 monks and 120 conversi, and at Louth Park 66 monks and 150 conversi. It was the intention that the conversi should perform all the necessary work both on the land and in the workshops, and that the convent should be self-supporting, the more educated looking after the farms and granges. As the Cistercian Order placed their houses in uncultivated and secluded valleys, the conversi were indispensable for tilling the land and bringing it into cultivation.

In the Gilbertine ordinances it states that the lay-brethren were admitted for novice probation at twenty-four years of age, and were immediately set to carting and other hard work, the master instructing them in religion and the rule. "The lay-brother should be ready to labour, in poor dress, content with the food of the poor. They reckoned herbs and pulses as riches and a draught of water was pleasant enough to those who dwelt in the granges." In summer they slept until after Lauds, as they had no midday rest, and a special bell was rung to wake them on account of their hard labour. They said their prayers and responses whilst at work and kept silence everywhere. When the light failed, one of the brothers struck a board, all ceased, said Compline and went to bed. The rule forbade anyone to hurt an animal in any way, but if a brother hurt himself by lifting too great a weight or by indiscreet and immoderate labour, he repented on bread and water or was beaten thrice in chapter. The poor dress St. Gilbert gave to the lay-brethren consisted of three white tunics, a grey cloth cloak lined with rough skins reaching to the thighs, a cope of cloth almost to the ground to wear in church, and a hood covering only the shoulders and chest. For carters, herdsmen and shepherds the prior might provide a fuller measure of cloth. He could give black shirts to the smiths, breeches to the carpenters and builders, and each had two pairs of gaiters and strong shoes made of the best leather to last a whole year.

The experiment of introducing the working class into monastic life was not an unqualified success, for they turned out to be unruly, turbulent and difficult to manage, those who looked after the farms appropriating the goods of the abbey. At Meaux in 1230, Abbot Richard Ottringham found it necessary to deal with the arrogance of the conversi in charge of the granges, and removed them, setting them to feed pigs, plough, joinery, stone-cutting, glazing and plumbing. At Evesham 1283–1316, Abbot Brockhampton found that certain brethren called conversi, whom his predecessor had placed in charge of the granges, had nearly demolished everything. They were recalled to perform their vows by fasting and

40 ROMSEY ABBEY, HAMPSHIRE (*Benedictine Nuns*): 12th-Century Transept Chapel

41 CHESTER ABBEY, NOW CATHEDRAL (*Benedictine*): the 15th-Century South Porch

42 TEWKESBURY ABBEY, GLOUCESTERSHIRE (*Benedictine*): looking East from the Norman Nave to the 14th-Century Quire

prayer. Again at the Augustinian priory at Gloucester, the Archbishop of York issued the following injunction in 1250: "that the canons are to have control of the conversi both within and without the monastery, and that no conversus is to have any authority over the canons." In the letter-book of Abbot Gregory of Whalley, who died in 1310, there is a letter sent to another house with a refractory conversus: "The bearer of this letter, a very strong wheelwright and a subtle lay-brother of our house, we have thought good to send to you, Father, with plenty of clothes, begging you earnestly to keep him and deal with him according to the discipline of our Order; that every Friday he is to have bread and water, and he is to be beaten at every chapter-meeting at which he is present until Easter, and for a year he is to eat no meat."

By the fourteenth century it was found better to farm out the land owing to its enhanced value, or to have the work done by hired servants, the Black Death giving the final blow to the continued existence of the conversi.

HIRED SERVANTS.—From the first the convents employed hired servants, and with the extinction of the conversi their use became general; in fact many houses indulged in this to extravagance and contained more servants than monks. At Durham in the sixteenth century there were over a hundred. At Evesham as early as 1090 there were 65 servants to 67 monks, and at Bury, 111 servants to 80 monks. At Gloucester in 1380 there were 200 officials and servants to 50 monks. The abbots of the greater monasteries kept large numbers of retainers, and the many attempts to check this were unavailing. The servants of a large house are divided by Snape under five heads: "(1st) artisans, smiths, carpenters, tilers, tailors, shoe-makers, etc.; (2nd) those engaged in the mill, bake-house, and brewery; (3rd) work within the grounds, gardeners, pig keepers, poultry and suchlike tasks; (4th) those at work in the stables and the messengers; (5th) servants within the house, the gate, the frater, kitchens, cellarer's department, laundry, farmery and the church." Much of the work of these men was intended by the founders to be done by the monks, but this ideal was early abandoned.

The fraterer, the chamberlain, the almoner and the master of the farmery had servants to help them, and the cellarer had several, the most important being the caterer who helped the kitchener. One Customal says "he ought to be broadminded and a strongminded man. One who acts with decision, and is wise, just, upright in all things belonging to his office; one who is prudent, knowing, discreet and careful when purchasing meat and fish in the markets." The caterer looked after the cook and his assistants, and at daily meals stood at the hatch and saw that things were served up in a fitting manner. He had two servants under him ready at his bidding to carry the provisions bought in the market. The abbot's cook held a similar position; he went each morning for his orders and had to see that the kitchener carried them out. He helped at great feasts and when there were many guests the work was heavy; if he needed help he could have a boy to run errands. "The larderer should be as perfect, just, faithful a servant as could be found. He had charge of the keys of the out-houses attached to the larder, the hay-house, the stockfish house and the pudding house." When the convent had baked meats, venison, turbot or eels, he had to prepare them for the cook. All live animals passed through his hands and he had to see to the killing, skinning and preparing of them for the spit. There were many cooks in the monastery besides the head cook and his assistants, those of the farmery and guest-house, the fish cook, the pittance cook, and the salter and bakers.

Many of these posts were hereditary possessions handed down from father to son. In some cases they were bought, as at Eynsham, where in 1280 John Ireton was appointed for life as head porter, with various allowances, for which he paid twenty pounds. At Dover the head porter was held for two generations by Valentine and Nicholas Bere, and included a corrody. The abbot, as has been stated, kept many servants, who were not always reliable. On the death of Abbot Hugh of Bury their character came out: "Ere he was dead, all things were thrown into disorder by the servants, so that in the abbot's house there was nothing at all left, except stools and tables which could not be carried away. There was hardly left for the abbot his coverlet and two quilts, old and torn, which someone who had taken the good ones had placed in their stead. There was not even a single article of a penny's worth that could be distributed amongst the poor for the good of his soul."

OTHER INHABITANTS.—Other people besides regulars and their servants lived in a monastery. The convents were in the habit of granting corrodies to persons who had benefited the house by gifts, land, influence or faithful service. The granting of a corrody came also as an expedient to help the funds when

43 HEXHAM PRIORY, NORTHUMBERLAND (*Augustinian*):
looking Northward across the 13th-Century Transepts

44 PERSHORE ABBEY, WORCESTERSHIRE (*Benedictine*):
the 13th-Century Quire, looking East

they were low. It was a method of insurance on the part of the holder, and of speculation on the part of the convent, but in the long run it did the finances of the abbey more harm than good. An abbot wishing to raise funds could sell a number of corrodies to obtain ready money, the convent having in the end to repay or buy them back. The receiver of a corrody was often allowed to have a room in the monastery with liberty of movement. There were two kinds granted, one in which the recipient obtained the same food as the monks, the other being provided from the servants' hall. The prior of Worcester granted to Richard de la Lynde, clerk, in 1308 "for as long as he lives, a room in the priory, with sufficient straw and firewood to be used when necessary in the fireplace; six pounds of candles of Paris tallow; twenty shillings a year of lawful money to be paid by the cellarer at Michaelmas. Every day of his life he will have one monk's loaf, one larger servant's loaf for his attendant, two gallons of superior beer, and one of servant's beer. Every day he will have pottage in quantity as a monk, and he will receive from the kitchen one dish of meat as a monk does, either cooked or raw as he prefers. For supper he will receive at the hatch allowance for two monks. He will have a stable near his room, with three cart-loads of hay, ten quarters of oats, also sixteen horse-shoes and nails." The above was for money lent. The next is for services to be rendered. It is granted to "Henry de Hampton, our clerk, for bestowing on us and our brethren for the future his advice, aid and service in the arts and practise of medicine." Snape quotes a similar one providing payment of a musician "to thump the organs and teach the quire boys, and instruct any of the monks who wish to learn the art of organ-thumping." Dr. Hunt points out that, as above, a corrody was not infrequently used as a means of paying wages. He quotes an instance in 1316 of the attachment of a plumber to Bath Abbey, who, being a villein, was manumitted in order to allow him to quit his holding, and then granted a corrody to do the convent's work. In 1316 Worcester granted a corrody to their architect or master-mason, William de Schokerwych, out of mere good will, but in exchange he placed sixty pounds of silver in their hands. There were corrodies which were harmful to the monastery; the patrons maintained the right to pension off their old retainers on the convent. Royalty formed no exception, and Dover under the King's patronage suffered. Edward III was no sooner on the throne than he installed John Pyk, yeoman of the King's buttery. In 1374 he pensioned off another old retainer, William Gardrobier, and in 1382 Oliver Marton, the King's serjeant.

Other persons, although not living within the monastery, enjoyed its protection. These were the sanctuary men, many abbeys enjoying that right. We gather from the correspondence relating to the suppression of Beaulieu that several families were under its protection. Quoting from the letters, "we find there are here sanctuary men for debt, felony and murder, thirty-two of them, many aged, some very sick; they have all of them wives and children and dwelling-houses and ground whereby they live. They have lamentably declared that if they are sent away, they shall be utterly undone. We have certain knowledge that the greater numbers of them should be utterly cast away, their age and impotence and other things considered." The late abbot pleaded for them that their behaviour was very honest, "and hath been all my time." Another letter states that "the miserable debtors far-steeped in age of long continuence, loden with wives and children must be compelled to beg and failing food dye of hunger. The whole inhabitants of Beaulieu, few excepted, be sanctuary men. The murderers and felons will incontinently and without further suit as hopeless men depart, the rest debtors of good behaviour and right quiet amongst their neighbours." It is satisfactory to know that these petitions ended in their being allowed to continue there for life.

CHAPTER III

THE MONASTERY

THE lives of those monks who were sent out from amongst their brethren to found new settlements were fraught with hardship and difficulty. When the monks from the abbey of St. Mary at York left their monastery in 1132, Archbishop Thurston assigned to them a dwelling place which afterwards came to be known as Fountains, "A place remote from all the world, uninhabited, set with thorns, and amongst the hollows of the mountains and prominent rocks, fit more, as it seemed, for the dens of wild beasts than for the uses of Mankind. Here the monks took up their abode, and spent the winter, their only shelter being a thatched hut round the stem of a great elm, and their food being provided for them by the good archbishop. During the day some occupied themselves in weaving mats, others in cutting twigs, whence an oratory might be built. During the following summer a great famine visited the district, and they were reduced to such straits that they cooked the leaves of the elm which had given them shelter." Meaux started as a two-storied building: the upper part the church, the lower inhabited by the monks until such times as permanent quarters could be provided. The majority of the first buildings were of timber and clay. When these came to be reconstructed in stone the eastern parts of the church were the first to be erected, including the presbytery, quire and transepts, together with the eastern side of the cloister, including the chapter-house and the dorter.

The church was the centre round which the monastery grew up, and the reason for its existence. It provided a fitting and adequate house where the worship of God could be carried out with dignity and ceremony. Its plan was a gradual development to meet the needs of the various rites which were added from time to time to the services of the church; such as the veneration of relics, the cult of the Virgin, and, as more monks became ordained, the provision of additional altars where they could each celebrate mass. The finished plan also provided a suitable setting for the spectacular processions which formed a prominent feature of Sundays and Festal-days.

The cruciform plan provided in its eastern limb the quire for the monks, with a presbytery beyond for the ceremonies connected with the high altar; the transepts for communication and additional altars; the nave for the use of the conversi or laymen. The Norman quire was of no great length, from two to four bays ending in an apse, the quire placed under the crossing and extending one or two bays into the nave. It was aisled on both sides, and in some instances the aisle was continued round the apse, forming a processional path, as can still be seen at Gloucester, Norwich, Tewkesbury and St. Bartholomew's, Smithfield (66). Its continuation allowed for the addition of radiating chapels (34); at Gloucester they are of two stories, the second reached from the triforium level. The general plan, however, was for the aisles to terminate in apsidal chapels; but with the lengthening of quires in later times these earlier arrangements have been obliterated. When the intercession of the Virgin became popular, chapels were built in her honour. At first they were erected alongside the church, on the south at Waltham and Worksop, on the north at Ely, Tewkesbury and Bristol, and at Wells in the cloister. Later they were constructed at the east-end beyond the presbytery. Many have been destroyed, but good examples remain at Winchester, Gloucester and Christchurch. Owing to circumstances one or two were built at the west-end as at Durham and Glastonbury.

With the coming of the Cistercians, their planning influenced the other Orders, and there was a return to the earlier English custom of square-ended quires. These were extended eastwards, occasionally being nearly the same length as the nave, and then the quire was withdrawn within the eastern limb. These extensions were necessitated by bringing the relics from the crypts into the churches, and the erection of costly shrines for their reception, usually placed in a feretory in the bay behind the great altar, as at Winchester (84). The Lady chapel at the east-end was generally the same height as the aisles, but in some instances, especially in the North, it was placed under the main roof, to the great advantage of the architectural setting, as at Beverley, Carlisle, Selby, Worcester and York. The Cistercians did not require Lady-chapels, as all their churches were dedicated to the Virgin and their houses built far from villages and towns.

As more altars were required, the processional path was

45 ABBEY DORE, HEREFORDSHIRE
(*Cistercian*): the Quire

46 ABBEY DORE, HEREFORDSHIRE
(*Cistercian*): the Eastern Chapels

47 BOXGROVE PRIORY, SUSSEX (*Benedictine*): the 13th-Century Quire, looking East

taken across the east-end behind the high altar, and a series of chapels erected against the east wall. At Abbey Dore (45, 46) the chapels and path formed a cross aisle beyond the east-end. This arrangement was developed at Fountains (7, 71) and Durham into an eastern transept the full height of the church, forming a fine architectural feature.

The quire of the monks was separated from the nave by a double screen, having a central doorway with altars on either side of it on its western face. This screen was called the pulpitum; from it at stated times the epistle and gospel were read, and the organs were housed upon it. It was generally constructed of stone, and took up a complete bay, having within it a staircase to reach the platform, although there is a wooden pulpitum at Hexham (74). The sides of the quire were protected by parclose screens, having doors on either side into the aisles of the quire. During the services the monks sat in wooden stalls, which commenced on either side of the pulpitum doorway, and continued on both sides of the quire. They were occupied in order of seniority, the abbot sitting immediately on the south side of the doorway and the prior on the north. Above the stalls were canopies to protect the heads of the brethren from the down draughts from the triforium and clerestory. These were designed from a simple covering to the wonderful spiring canopies of the fifteenth and sixteenth centuries (73, 75); unfortunately many sets were wantonly destroyed at the suppression. At Roche Abbey "the persons that cast the lead into fodders, plucked up all the seats in the quire, wherein the monks sat when they said service, which were like the seats in minsters, and burned them, and melted the lead wherewithal; although there was wood plenty within a flight shot of them, for the abbey stood amongst the woods and rocks of stone." In the middle of the quire stood a great lectern, where, as at Durham, "the monks did sing their legends at matins and other times."

One transept had a doorway leading to the monks' burial ground, the other contained the night-stairs from the dorter, the best remaining example being at Hexham (98). The transepts also provided additional space for altars. In Norman times there were one or at the most two apsidal chapels on their eastern side, as at Romsey (40). The first Cistercian transepts had a series of chapels, separated by solid walls and with individual stone roofs, as at Fountains, Kirkstall, Buildwas and originally Furness. In later times the transepts were aisled on their eastern sides containing three or four chapels, divided by parclose screens of wood or stone. The quire and transepts being private to the convent were shut away by screens, and as the quire extended one or two bays into the nave, these enclosed the eastern processional cloister doorway. The central screen, of which a stone example remains at St. Albans (77) and a wooden one at Dunstable (76), formed the rood-screen, over which the great Rood was either placed or hung. Unlike the pulpitum it had a central nave altar with doorways on either side. The bay between the two screens was used by the infirm monks, who could not stand through the long services. It is probable that the medieval bench preserved at Winchester (p. 21) was used for this purpose.

In the construction of a church the nave was always the last portion to be erected. In the various rebuildings which took place it seems in some cases never to have been completed. At the suppression Bristol, Hexham and Milton Abbas (8) lacked their naves, while Kelso and Sawley were little better than ante-chapels to the quires. Monastic naves varied in planning. Many were aisleless, as Lilleshall, and when in later years aisles were added, the side against which the cloister was built could not be used, resulting in many naves having but one aisle. The naves of Cistercian houses were of extreme length and were used for the services of the conversi, low walls being built between the piers of the arcades, shutting away the aisles except in the western bay, which was always left open. When the conversi were dispersed, the intervening walls were removed and chapels and chantries introduced. The nave had, in addition to the western processional cloister doorway, a western portal used for special occasions and festivals. Its absence is rare, but examples may be cited at Brinkburn, Buildwas, Cartmel, Furness and Romsey. A further doorway was provided near the west end on the side farthest from the cloister for the use of laymen. This was often covered by a porch; an early example remains at Malmesbury and later ones at Canterbury, Chester (41), Gloucester and Malvern. In Augustinian and Benedictine churches the nave was sometimes parochial and has been retained when all else has been destroyed.

When a parish had the right of worship within a monastic church, the parishioners were often provided with an aisle, as the north aisle at Crowland and the south aisles at Leominster and Blyth which were enlarged for that purpose. At Cartmel

48 SHREWSBURY ABBEY (*Benedictine*): the new East End

49 SHERBORNE ABBEY, DORSET (*Benedictine*): looking East

50 DORCHESTER PRIORY, OXFORDSHIRE (*Benedictine*):
the 14th-Century Quire, looking East

the south aisle of the quire was widened for their use. Two services in the one church at the same time could never have been satisfactory, and led to continual quarrels and unpleasantness. At Sherborne a parish church was built butting on the west end of the monastic church. By keeping the font in the monastic nave the monks compelled the parishioners to be baptised by them, and an arch from the monastic to the parish church was constructed for this purpose; by lessening the arch to a doorway the monks incensed the populace, which led to the shooting of lighted arrows into the thatch which was protecting the rebuilding of the monks' church whereby it was burnt down. There was also trouble at Chester. The convent, wishing to enlarge the church, and the south transept being the only part available, they pulled down a parish church which stood in the way; the parishioners therefore claimed the right to worship in the new transept. This became so vexatious that the monks built them a new church without the precincts, which they refused to use, and they continued in the transept until well into the nineteenth century. During a quarrel at Wymondham a wall was erected upon the roodscreen completely shutting off the nave, but the quarrel continued over the bells, the parishioners finally building their own steeple. The solution at Evesham and many other monasteries was in the erection of separate chapels.

As the eastern transept for additional altars was a thirteenth-century innovation, so the western transept belonged to the twelfth century. Western transepts existed at St. Edmundsbury, Peterborough and Ely. This feature, surmounted with tall corner turrets and combined with a great single western tower, formed a fine architectural façade. St. Edmundsbury has been destroyed and the later front at Peterborough masks the real planning behind it, but Ely still remains, bereft of its northern wing. The western doorways at Peterborough and Ely are covered by porches, and the Cistercians also masked their western portals with a lean-to narthex, which remains in part at Fountains, and of which there are indications at Byland.

Towers played an important part in the general design of monastic churches. They varied in position and number, a single tower over the crossing, or two by the addition of one at the west end, or three, one central and two western. At first the central towers were low, as at Winchester and Romsey, and were surmounted by a pyramidal roof as at Boxgrove. Later, additional stories were added upon foundations not intended to receive them. This was the cause of so many downfalls and rebuildings. When the central tower was combined with two western towers a fine effect was produced as at Canterbury and Durham. Many western towers remain when the central ones have been destroyed, as at Bourn, Bridlington and Worksop (14). The Cistercians were forbidden towers; but as the rules relaxed, they too built them, as at Kirkstall (28). At Fountains, after trying in vain to build a central tower on insecure foundations, they erected a stately steeple at the end of the north transept (2, 7).

FOUNTAINS: REMAINS OF THE NARTHEX
BEFORE THE WEST DOOR OF THE CHURCH

Although the church, and the continual contemplation and worship of God was the sole reason for the existence of a monastery, lodgings had to be provided for the worshippers, or else worship ceased. These offices were ranged round the four sides of a more or less square garth or lawn, and between the buildings and the garth were four alleyways with a pentice roof, where the monks lived when not in church or attending to other affairs. At first the cloister, as it was termed, was unprotected from the weather, the walls being open colonnades looking upon the garth, as at Newminster (87). This in a warm climate such as Italy might be pleasant, but in England with its changeable climate and cold winters it proved alto-

51 ROMSEY ABBEY, HAMPSHIRE (*Benedictine Nuns*):
the Interior, looking East

52 AUSTIN FRIARS, LONDON: the Nave, built for Preaching

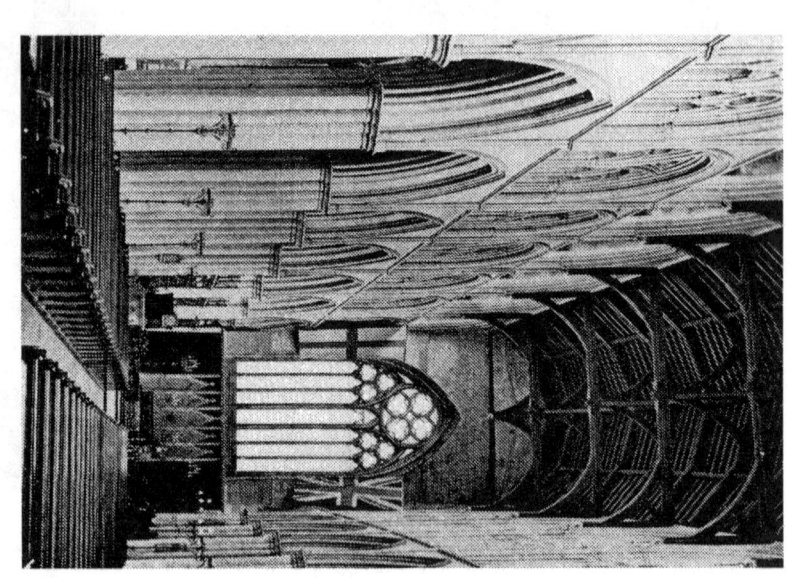

53 BRIDLINGTON PRIORY, YORKSHIRE (*Augustinian*): Only the 14th-Century Nave remains

THE MONASTERY

gether too austere for the brethren, and the cloister walls were eventually built in with a series of windows, as at Lacock (90) and Westminster (85), which were glazed. Even then they remained unheated and were sufficiently cold and draughty. In England, when the situation allowed, they were planned on the south side of the church to obtain as much warmth and sunshine as possible, the buildings shielding them from the north and east winds. When this was not possible, especially when the town impinged upon the monastery, as at Canterbury and Gloucester, or where, as at Chester, the abbey occupied the north-east corner of the walled city, the cloister was built on the north side to be as far away as possible from noise.

In general, the planning of the cloistral buildings was common to most of the Orders, although it might differ in its setting out. The alley against the church, whether north or south, was the one principally occupied by the brethren. The wall against the garth was divided into carrels or small closets for study, each taking up the space of half a window. These were partitioned off by wainscoting, wherein was a desk for the books, enough space being left behind the carrels to form a corridor. Carrels can be seen at Gloucester (112), where the stonework remains, and at Chester, where they have been reconstructed. Sometimes stone benching was provided against the wall of the church, and each end of the alley was enclosed by a wooden screen. The books were kept in an aumbry built in the wall by the processional doorway in the east alley. At Chester there are six arches in the south alley which contained book-cupboards. At Furness they stood in closets entered by arches on either side of the chapter-house doorway, and there are the remains of one at Valle Crucis in the form of a window. It was not, however, until later that the greater monasteries assigned a separate room for the library, as at Gloucester and Durham.

On the east side of the cloister came first the west wall of the south transept in which the book-cupboard was placed. Between the transept and the chapter-house was the usual position for the slype or passage to the monks' cemetery. It was also used as the common-room, where the rule of silence was relaxed and the brethren were allowed to see visitors, the key being kept by the sub-prior. The slype at Gloucester (89) has a range of arcading along one side forming seats, and at St. Albans there are remains of an elaborate arcading, once part of the slype. If the slype was placed further south, its original position was used for a dual purpose, the portion against the cloister being the treasury, and the inner half a sacristy opening into the church, as at Valle Crucis. At Durham the treasury occupied a similar position in the west alleyway.

VALLE CRUCIS: LIBRARY CUPBOARD

Of the buildings connected with the east cloister the most important was the chapter-house with the dorter above it. It was next in dignity to the church, and in early times was considered sufficiently sacred to be used as the burial place of the dignitaries of the house; sometimes the bodies of the brethren reposed there on their way to their last resting-place. In construction the chapter-house varied more than any other

54 MONKS CHANTING THE OFFICE OF THE DEAD

*MS. Egerton 1070 fol. 54 rev.,
British Museum*

part of the monastery. It was designed on plan either oblong, square, apsidal, polygonal, or an aisled hall, the latter being a feature of Cistercian houses. If the chapter-house rose to the full height of the range it shortened the dorter above, but the usual custom was to approach it through a vestibule, which enabled it to be designed to the wishes of the abbot or master-mason. Many of these houses are amongst the gems of their periods, and examples may be seen in the vestibules at Bristol and Chester (96), the entrances to Furness and Haughmond (91), the pillared halls of Lacock (92), and Valle Crucis (95) and the polygonal chapter-houses at Cockersand, Westminster and Worcester. Many have been destroyed, including Carlisle, Dore, Evesham and Margam, but we can still study the type in the secular examples at Lincoln, Salisbury, Southwell, Wells and York; even a simple room in the small priory at Birkenhead is charming (93).

The dorter was built over the eastern range and generally extended for its whole length. Between it and the transept was a vestibule, situated above the slype, and from it descended the night-stairs into the church, the best example being at Hexham (98). When the chapter-house took up the full height of the range, a passage was often left whereby to reach the stairs; otherwise the day-stairs were used. Although at Furness the chapter-house had a vestibule, the dorter extended over both. The day-stairs were situated according to convenience. A fine fourteenth-century example remains at Chester (99). In small abbeys they were often cramped in an awkward way, as at Valle Crucis, where they are built into the side of the chapter-house wall. Circular stairs were also used, as at Chester and St. Radegund's, Bradsole, where one is built in the south-west corner of the transept, serving as both day- and night-stairs.

Several dorters retain their roofs and are now used for other purposes. Those at Durham (97) and Westminster are libraries. Those at Cleeve and Valle Crucis were used by later inhabitants for domestic purposes; that at Forde now forms part of a private mansion, cut into smaller rooms. In early times the dorter was open from end to end, the beds ranged with their heads to the wall, leaving a gangway down the centre. Later, partitions were used, either in the form of curtains or wainscoting, to give greater privacy. Attached to the dorter by a bridge was another building known as the rere-dorter or necessarium. It was a long narrow building, with a row of seats against the wall, each with its own window, and divided by partitions. Beneath, walled in, was a drain, either artificially cut or a natural stream diverted. At Furness the seats were ranged back to back in a long double row. These buildings were of considerable length, Canterbury being 145 feet and Lewes 158 feet. The undercroft beneath the dorter was utilised in various ways in different monasteries. A passage to the infirmary often ran through it, and the rest

DRAINAGE SYSTEM TO LAVATORY, GLOUCESTER

included the calefactory or warming room, where a fire was kept burning night and day from All Saints until Easter, being the only warmth kept for the monks, apart from those who were ill. It was customarily situated beneath the dorter, even when in special cases the dorter did not occupy its ordinary position. At Gloucester the dorter was at right angles to the cloister owing to the cramped space, and at Durham it was finally placed over the western range. In both cases the warming room was beneath it. In Cistercian houses the calefactory was placed next to the frater, as is to be found at Fountains (111). Few monasteries were planned exactly alike in detail, and to discover the various deviations from the

55 EWENNY PRIORY, GLAMORGANSHIRE (*Benedictine*): the Quire Barrel Vault

56 BLYTH ABBEY, NOTTINGHAMSHIRE (*Benedictine*): the North Quire Aisle, showing the early vaulting

57 HINTON CHARTERHOUSE, SOMERSET
(*Carthusian*) : the Chapter-house

58 WOODSPRING PRIORY, SOMERSET
(*Augustinian*) : now used as a dwelling-house

general plan makes a visit to a ruined abbey all the more interesting.

The frater flanked the alleyway opposite the church, except in Cistercian houses, and ran parallel with the church, the door being at its western end. In many places it was built upon an undercroft, as at Westminster and Gloucester; in others on the ground floor, as at Chester. Few fraters remain, those at Chester and Worcester being exceptions. The frater was a hall of considerable size, oblong in shape and was entered through screens; there were buttery hatches

BASINGWERK ABBEY: KITCHEN HATCH TO FRATER

for the passing of food from the kitchens as at Basingwerk, and it also had aumbries for the silver and napery. Its two outstanding features were the reader's pulpit, and a representation of the Rood on the east wall above the head of the presiding officer. Remains of these may be seen at Cleeve and Worcester. The pulpit in the greater monasteries was built out from the wall on the south side, with stairs constructed in the thickness of the wall. The best examples are to be found at Beaulieu (108) and Chester; at Shrewsbury the pulpit (109) alone remains, all else being destroyed. The Cistercian refectory differed in many respects and was built out at right-angles to the cloister and ordinarily on the ground floor. Owing to the popularity of the Order it could therefore be enlarged as required.

Excellent fraters remain in a ruined state at Fountains (103) and Rievaulx (104), the latter built upon an undercroft owing to the rapid fall of the ground; Beaulieu has been mentioned; at Cleeve the frater was rebuilt on an undercroft in the fifteenth century (106) and retains its roof (107). When thus built it allowed of a passage from the cloister to the outer court, which still exists at Westminster. Meat was forbidden in the frater, but as the rule was slackened permission was granted for the brethren to eat it on three days of the week; this necessitated a special room. First the farmery misericord was used, but later, rooms were built for the purpose, and meals in the frater became increasingly unpopular. At Durham there was a loft set apart as a misericord; frequently the frater was divided up, but more often it was rebuilt, the upper storey as the frater, the lower as the misericord. This plan was adopted at Furness, Kirkstall and Ford, all Cistercian houses. At Jervaulx a room was built out at right-angles to the east end of the old frater, and at Westminster parallel to the old hall.

FOUNTAINS: PULPIT STAIRS IN FRATER

The kitchens were closely connected with the frater, and in Benedictine houses were built outside the cloister. Two kitchens of the greater monasteries remain, one at Glastonbury (110) and the other at Durham; they are square on plan with fireplaces in the angles, the arches supporting octagonal vaulted roofs, the smoke being taken by flues to a central louvre. At Haughmond (113), the large chimneys of the more ordinary type of kitchen remain. In addition to the fires there were also ovens, as well as copper cauldrons with fires beneath them, and a chute for the disposal of rubbish. In Cistercian

59 WESTMINSTER ABBEY, LONDON (*Benedictine*): the Nave, looking East

60 WESTMINSTER ABBEY, LONDON (*Benedictine*): the Chapel of Henry VII

houses the kitchen came within the cloister between the frater and the buildings connected with the conversi, so that meals could be served to both from the same place. At Fountains the fires were placed back to back in the centre of the room; a door into the cloister made it easy to obtain the provisions from the cellarer's checker. In Cistercian houses the brethren did their own cooking; therefore the admission of the kitchen into the cloister was of no importance.

Connected with the frater was the lavatory for the washing of hands and faces before meals. It usually consisted of a stone trough set back in the frater wall and not impinging on the cloister walk, and close by was the recess for the towels. Many lavatories remain in a more or less ruinous condition, as at Chester, Haughmond, Worcester and Norwich (101). At times they were an architectural feature, as at Gloucester (105), where the lavatory runs parallel to the side of the cloister, the towel recess being on the opposite side of the walk (p. 51). At Much Wenlock, Durham and Canterbury the lavatories were separate buildings placed in the garth; Canterbury (p. 50) remains, and there are fragments of the one at Wenlock, which was constructed of marble with carved panels. Of the Durham lavatory there is a description in the *Rites of Durham*. "Within the cloister garth over against the frater-house was a fair laver or conduit for the monks to wash their hands and faces at, being made in round form covered with lead, and all of marble saving the very uttermost walls. Within the walls you may walk round about the laver of marble having many little conduits or spouts of brass with twenty-three cocks of brass round about it, having in it seven fair windows of stonework, and in the top a fair dovecote, covered evenly above with lead, the workmanship both fine and costly as is apparent to this day. And adjoining to the east side of the conduit door, there did hang a bell to give warning, at eleven of the clock, for the monks to come and wash and dine, having the closet or aumbries, on either side of the frater door, kept always with sweet and clean towels as is aforesaid to dry their hands."

The western range was usually on the side next to the outer court, to which it had access by a slype situated between the undercroft and the church; this was used as the outer parlour where the convent transacted business with merchants and layfolk in connection with the affairs of the monastery. The remainder of the undercroft was divided into offices, the

DETAIL OF LAVATORY BASIN, MUCH WENLOCK PRIORY

61 CHRISTCHURCH PRIORY, HAMPSHIRE (*Augustinian*): a Peep into the Quire, showing the Reredos and Salisbury Chantry

62 CARTMEL PRIORY, LANCASHIRE (*Augustinian*): looking towards the Quire. Late 12th Century

principal being the cellarer's checker together with the buttery. The upper floor was assigned as the abbot's guest-hall, the remainder of his lodgings being built out from it. The Cister-

TOWEL CUPBOARD IN CLOISTER, GLOUCESTER

cian western range was devoted to the needs of the conversi, being separated from the west alley by an intervening passage or yard. At Fountains (117) the fine undercroft of twenty-two bays is double aisled. It was formerly divided by a slype near the kitchens, which formed the outer parlour and entrance from the cloister to the outer court. South of this was the frater of the conversi. On the north the sub-vault was divided into cellars for the cellarer's checker, which was entered from the outer court, over which ran a long wooden pentice. The upper storey formed the dorter of the conversi (116), from which a night-stair led directly into the nave of the church, the day-stair being on the western side of the outer court. When the conversi were dispersed, these buildings were put to other uses, often as the abbots' lodgings.

Of the claustral buildings outside the cloister garth, the most important was the farmery. It was generally situated on the east side of the cloisters and connected with it by a covered alleyway. This group of buildings included the infirmary hall, chapel, misericord and kitchen. The layout was dictated by the space at the disposal of the monastery. The main hall was planned as a church, with arcades, aisles and sometimes clerestories, the chapel at the end forming a chancel. The parish church at Ramsey is thought to have been the infirmary hall of the monastery. In lesser houses a simplified plan was adopted, which was also used for hospitals unconnected with monasteries, as St. Mary's hospital at Chichester. The beds were placed in the aisles with their heads to the wall. If no remains of fireplaces can be found in the ruins it can be assumed that there was a central fire, the smoke escaping through a louvre in the roof. In later times the aisles were divided into separate chambers, and sometimes small rooms were built out from the sides of the hall.

At Westminster, when the farmery was rebuilt, instead of a hall, a series of small chambers were built round a little cloister where the convalescent and decrepit monks could walk and sit. There were other occupants in addition to the sick; the old and infirm and, in Cistercian houses, those who had been professed for over fifty years. The brethren who were periodically bled were allowed in the farmery and given better food. In the earlier days they did not fare as well; in 1090 Abbot Paul of St. Albans said "that instead of feeding on meat pasties they should have a dish of salt fish." The farmery had its own kitchen where meat could be cooked, which was served in the misericord; and it was to this hall that the monks came when they were allowed meat on three days a week. In Cistercian houses there was a separate farmery for the conversi, situated in the outer court, as at Fountains.

THE MONASTERY

The early ordinance that the abbot and prior should sleep in the dorter was soon abandoned, but a semblance of the rule was provided by a corridor connecting the dorter to the abbot's lodging. Later this was also given up, and a new building apart from the monks was erected. In the Benedictine Order this was placed against the west cloister, as at Chester, Gloucester and Westminster. It occupies the same site at Ely and is now used for the deanery. Near by is the prior's chapel, erected by John of Crauden (121). At Furness the old farmery was reconditioned for the abbot's lodging, and examples may be found in almost any part of the monastic courtyard. As the abbots and priors entertained the more notable guests, larger halls and several rooms had to be provided. At Westminster the abbot's lodging surrounds a small courtyard with the dining-hall on the west, and the kitchen adjoining its southern end. On the north against the church are the Jerusalem and Jericho parlours, and the lodgings were continued between the western cloister and the courtyard. At the suppression many of these houses were adapted to the needs of the new owners and have been in part preserved, as the hall at Ford and the prior's lodging at Wenlock (120). Other remains are to be found at Watton (118), Castle Acre (119), and Muchelney (123).

In the outer court stood the guest-house, the almonry, brewery, bakehouse, granary and workshops. The same division of the guests seems to have been followed in all monasteries. The nobles were entertained by the abbot or prior, ordinary travellers by the hosteller in the guest-house, and the poor in the almonry. The two last-named buildings were close to the gate-house. Not many now remain, but the guest-house of Dover priory is now used as the school chapel, whilst the fine Norman porch at Canterbury (127) was once the entrance to the almonry; a timber-built almonry still exists at Evesham (129).

The gate-houses of monasteries have often been preserved. An important abbey had more than one entrance and there was a second or inner gate when there were two courtyards. The early examples show but a single arch, but in later types a wicket or postern was added for foot-passengers. On one side was the porter's lodge and the upper storey was sometimes used as a chapel. Perhaps the finest example remains at Thornton, constructed of brick with stone quoins; this was military as well as domestic, with barbicans (132). Many others are imposing, as the gates at St. Edmundsbury (130), Battle (134), St. Osyths (133), Kirkham (p. 78), and Worksop (135). They descended in the architectural scale to the timber and stone gateways at Wigmore, Bromfield and Evesham (129).

Monasteries possessed many buildings outside their walls. Often a school was provided, either in connection with the almonry or distinct from it. In 1213 the prior of Bermondsey founded a hospital for poor boys which was built against the

ST. LEONARD'S CHAPEL FROM S.W., KIRKSTEAD, LINCS.
THIRTEENTH CENTURY

outer walls of the courtyard. In 1331 the abbot of St. Augustine, Canterbury, built a school without the gates for poor boys, and there were schools in the almonries at Durham, Barnwell and St. Albans. Almshouses and lay infirmaries were general. At Glastonbury twelve poor women were maintained, at Durham four aged women, and at Reading thirteen poor persons were fed and clothed in almshouses. The "capella-extra-portas," or chapel without the gate, was a customary feature. It was used by women and persons who were not permitted within the precincts, and sometimes became the village church as at Whitegate, Cheshire. The chapel at

63 BRINKBURN PRIORY, NORTHUMBERLAND (*Augustinian*):
Looking East. Late 12th Century

64 LLANTHONY PRIORY, MONMOUTHSHIRE (*Augustinian*):
looking East

65 BUILDWAS ABBEY, SHROPSHIRE (*Cistercian*): looking
East. Late 12th Century

Merevale is still in use as the parish church; others remain at Coggeshall and Kirkstead. There were also chapels for pilgrims on the roads leading to monasteries possessing wonder-working relics, as the beautiful chapel at Houghton-le-dale on the road to Walsingham, that of which the tower alone remains on the Tor at Glastonbury, and St. Catherine's chapel at Abbotsbury. Inns were also provided for pilgrims, and remain at Gloucester and Glastonbury.

There were many other buildings connected with the management of an abbey, but time and neglect have destroyed most of them. At Glastonbury is a stone building known as the tribunal (124), where the abbot's court was held to try offenders who came under his jurisdiction. Near Chester is Saighton Grange formerly owned by the abbey of Chester (122), and there are a few tythe-barns belonging to monastic estates such as Bradford-on-Avon (126), Abbotsbury and Torre.

The planning of the Carthusian monastery was individual to that Order; it was not so much a community as a gathering of anchorites, and the only place in England where it can be studied is Mount Grace in Yorkshire. The plan consisted of two courts, the cloister being the northern one, surrounded on three sides by separate cells with small gardens attached. Separating the two courts were the cells of the prior and sacrist, together with the chapter-house and fratery. Behind the chapter-house stood the church, entered by a covered passage. The southern or outer court had several cells near the church, the rest being occupied by store-houses, the guest-house and the gateway.

CHAPTER IV

THE DAILY LIFE

ALTHOUGH the hours of service and the type of work differed a little in the various Orders, the life in general was common to all. A monk's year was divided into summer and winter, the former extending from Easter to the middle of September. His day was the natural day from sunrise to sunset, and consisted of twelve hours, varying in length according to the seasons, although it actually began at midnight when the first and longest service of the day took place.

The sacrist and his assistants together with the sub-prior were up early to prepare the church and convent for this nightly vigil. Awakened by the sub-prior ringing the bell in the dorter, the brethren crossed themselves, rose and put on the parts of their habits in which they had not slept, together with their night boots of soft leather, said their prayers, and waited seated upon their beds with their heads covered in their hoods, until one of the bells tolled softly. They then proceeded down into the quire, a junior carrying a lantern before them to show the way.

In the quire the juniors occupied the stalls nearest the altar, the seniors those furthest away. The abbot and prior stood without the door until all had passed in before them, and then gave the signal for the bell to cease. Their coming into the quire was signalised by all rising from their knees and returning their salutation, and at once they repeated the triple-prayer and the gradual psalms, at which every one had to be present. At the end, those officials who had other duties to perform might retire, and the second ringing of the bells announced the commencement of Matins. At the beginning of the lessons the appointed reader fetched a candle, mounted the lectern steps, and held it so that the light fell upon the place of his reading, each lesson being read by a different brother. On the feast of the twelve lessons the preparations for the service were made during the singing of the *Te Deum*, servants bringing in a portable lectern, others the cope and vestments of the colour of the day, and the sacrist with great solemnity bringing the gospels from the altar. He then conducted the priest to the desk, vested him in his cope and

66 ST. BARTHOLOMEW'S PRIORY, LONDON (*Augustinian*):
Norman Apsidal Quire

67 ST. BOTOLPH'S PRIORY, COLCHESTER, ESSEX (*Augustinian*):
the Remains of the Nave

68 NETLEY ABBEY, HAMPSHIRE (*Cistercian*):
View from South Transept

pointed out the place for him to read, whilst the servers brought in the incense and lights. The priest then chanted the appointed gospels and finished with the prayers for the day, the bells being immediately rung for Lauds. During the interval the lantern over the great lectern was trimmed, the monks either remaining in their places or taking a walk in the cloisters to restore circulation. When the bell had ceased, the second service commenced, and at its conclusion between

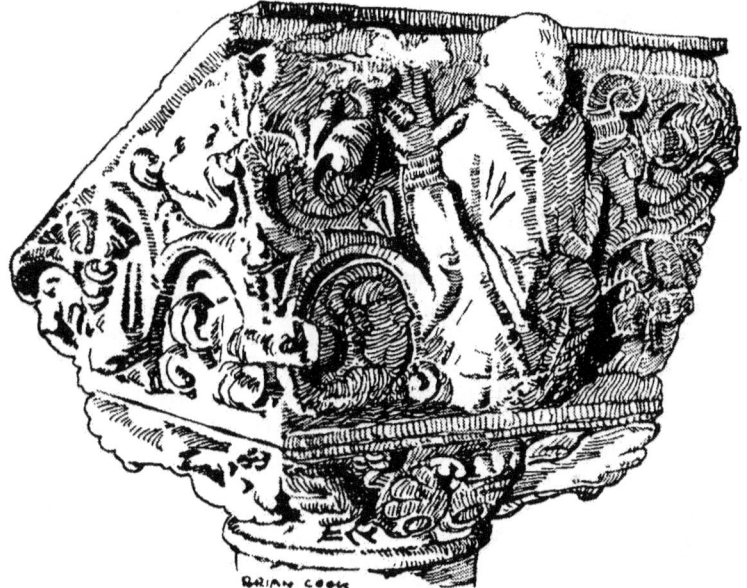

STONE LECTERN, NORTON

one and two o'clock the monks returned in procession to the dorter, led as before by a junior with a lantern. They then partook of their second sleep. During these early services the circator went round the church with a lantern to see that no brother was overcome by drowsiness. If he found one he placed the lantern before his eyes and shook him, returning to his own place. The brother had then to take up the lantern, until he also found a brother in like condition when the same thing was repeated. The church was dimly lighted by a few candles, and, as the brethren had been roused from their first sleep, drowsiness would be difficult to resist.

They were again awakened at daybreak by the ringing of

a bell, and, dressed in their day clothes, were seated in quire before the bell stopped. Prime was not a long service, but immediately after it the great bell rang for the early mass intended for the servants and workpeople at which the convent was not bound to attend. The brethren went into the cloister, washed themselves and combed their hair. There are careful directions how this was to be done, "the brethren were not to blow their noses on the towels or to remove dirt with them." The senior priests then prepared to say their private masses, others took books into the cloister, and there read and sang in an undertone, the novices going to their appointed place to be taught. Before the next service, should it not be a fast day, the brethren were allowed some slight refreshment, called mixtum, consisting of a quarter of a pound of bread and a third of a pint of beer or wine, taken standing in the refectory. During this, the first bell was kept ringing for morning mass, known either as the Lady-mass because it was celebrated in the Lady-chapel, or as chapter-mass because it immediately preceded morning chapter. The monks assembled in cloister, and as the second bell tolled, moved into the church in procession. The mass was said in a low audible voice with no particular ceremonial. On its conclusion the great bell rang for the daily chapter. During its ringing the brethren remained in their stalls, the officials consulting together in the private parlour over matters calling for notice, the custodian of the cloisters seeing that all the doors were locked so that no one could enter during chapter.

The juniors went first in the order of procession into the chapter-house, and all stood and bowed as the abbot passed through them. The prior then came forward and kissed his hand, bowing before and after the ceremony. When all had taken their seats, one of the brethren went into the pulpit and read aloud the martyrology for the day; continuing, the priest for the week read certain psalms and collects, followed by the portion of the rule assigned for the day, and by briefs of the death of persons in whom the convent was interested. The tables were then read on which were written the names of those brethren who were responsible for the weekly duties. Next came a sermon, usually preached by the head of the house, after which the novices, lay-brethren and strangers took their leave. The chapter then devoted themselves to the correction of faults. First a brother could confess and ask for forgiveness; then the circator made his statement of what

69 FURNESS ABBEY, LANCASHIRE (*Cistercian*) : View into the Quire

70 SELBY ABBEY, YORKSHIRE (*Benedictine*): the Nave Arcade, showing the gradual change in Styles

he had seen and heard whilst going the rounds of the house; finally the accusations made by one monk against another were heard. The accused was allowed to make no defence or excuses; but no brother was to accuse another on mere suspicion, only on what he had seen and heard. After the accusations the abbot pronounced his punishment, and the penance generally took some form of corporal chastisement. If it was desirable to have the accused flogged, he was not to be flogged by his accuser, only by an equal or a superior; he was to rise to his knees and modestly divest himself of his garments as far as his girdle, and he who flogged him was not to cease until the abbot bade him; he was then to help the brother to put on his clothes. It should be remembered that flagellation was a well-recognised form of religious devotion and was largely followed apart from the monastic Orders.

After accusations the convent considered the temporal business connected with the house, the sealing of charters, the admission of novices or the commemoration of the departed. Should the chapter prove short and there be an interval before the next service, the brethren had leave to talk in the cloister until the bell rang for Tierce. In some monastic houses this time was spent in a different manner, a part of the cloister being set apart for the monks' parliament, the abbot or prior being ready to hear those who sought for guidance, or had business to transact with officials, also to discuss matters of policy or points of difficulty connected with the rule. In another part the senior monks met to hear a devotional reading and discuss it afterwards, and in the western alley the novices together with two or three seniors asked questions about the observances or cited perplexing passages for their interpretation, ordinary conversation not being allowed.

At the ringing of a bell all books were put away and the brethren prepared themselves for the next service, which was high mass. On this occasion the stalls nearest the altar were occupied by the senior monks. If Tierce had not already been said it was the first hour to be taken, and during it preparations were made for the blessing of the water. On Sundays and Festal-days at this point of the service the procession round the church and cloister took place. Dinner followed mass, the brethren coming out of church in procession, first going to the lavatory to wash their hands and faces, sharpen their knives and brush their hair. If dinner was ready they went straight into the frater, but if not they stood without the frater doorway. An injunction at Ely states "that if the monks persisted in holding their parliaments at the door of the frater or near it, they were to be put on bread and water until they promised better obedience." This being the first meal of the day the brethren would be inclined to grumble and be impatient if it was unduly delayed. The Superior and his guests sat at the east end on a raised dais under the great Rood, the brethren at tables ranged down the sides of the room with their backs to the wall, but at a sufficient distance to enable the servitors to pass behind them. During the meal conversation was forbidden, and from the frater pulpit the monk appointed read suitable portions from the lives of the saints or other homilies in a slow distinct voice, repeating any passage he considered sufficiently important. "The brethren ought not to be noisy during the reading. If some had nuts, they were not to crack them with their teeth, but open them quietly with their knives so as not to disturb the reader; if however everyone had nuts they might crack them at will without considering him." Nothing very definite is said as to the quality of the meals provided. There were two courses; the dietary was to be always so plentiful and good as to do away with all excuses for dining at private houses or inns. The monks could ask for every sort of fish, vegetables, pastry, fruit, cheese, wine, water or milk. Spices, figs, ale and cakes were annually provided for Lent, and the never-failing pork-pies, capons, fig-tarts and blanc-mange of rice and almonds appeared at Festivals. Beer was the common drink of the convent, or it would not have been a hardship to be put on bread and water.

It is possible to form some idea of the food of the convent from various kitchen bills which have been preserved. At Winchester on Good Friday, 1515, harburden, red herrings, minnows as *entrée*, and mustard were provided. On Easter Sunday, being a feast day, the menu contained spiced vegetables, meat pudding, 340 eggs, venison as *entrée*, fish ground with crumbs as pittance dish, broth, open tarts, beef and mutton. At Dover in 1530, one week's kitchen bill included mutton, lamb, geese and capons, oysters, plaice, whilkes, salt salmon and fresh fish, butter and eggs.

There were many directions as to behaviour in frater; "the brethren ought to eat what is set before them temperately, cleanly and cheerfully; they ought to speak sparingly, and **not**

71 FOUNTAINS ABBEY, YORKSHIRE (*Cistercian*): the 13th-Century Chapel of the Nine Altars, looking North

72 LASTINGHAM PRIORY, YORKSHIRE (*Benedictine*):
12th-Century Crypt beneath the Quire

73 FROM WHALLEY ABBEY, LANCASHIRE (*Cistercian*): the Canopied Stalls, now in the Parish Church

74 HEXHAM PRIORY, NORTHUMBERLAND (*Augustinian*):
the Wooden Pulpitum

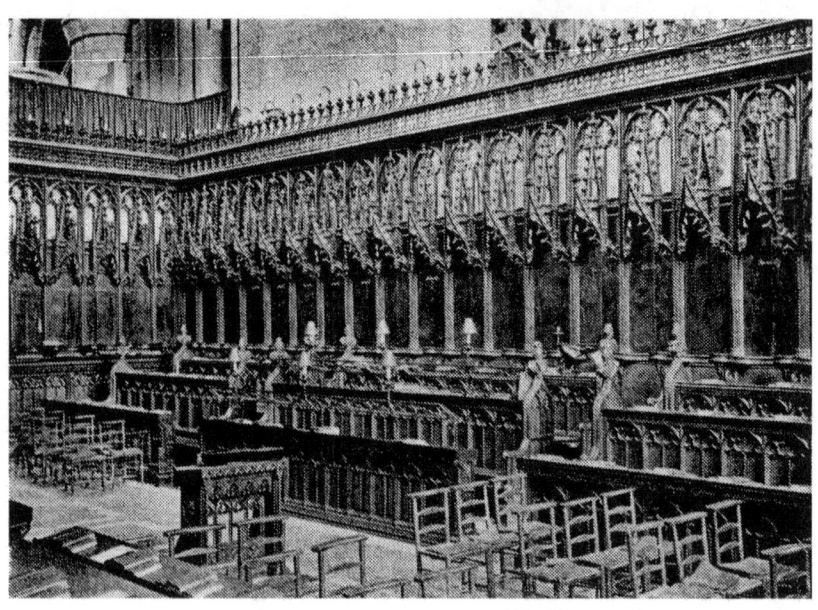

75 GLOUCESTER CATHEDRAL ABBEY (*Benedictine*):
the Canopied Stalls

let their eyes wander. A monk was not to sit chin in hand, or spread his hands across his face; each brother should sit up straight and keep his arms off the table. He was not to wipe his teeth on the table-cloth, or cut or wipe the table-cloth with his knife. When soft fruit was served, it should be placed in bowls to prevent the table-cloths from being stained." Spoons were provided, the brethren using their own knives; forks being unknown, they used their hands. "Those who served the brethren ought not to rush about nor stand aimlessly in one place, nor gossip with the kitchen servers even about the dishes they received." Extra rations or pittance were also given to the monks at stated times, but dining in the frater was not popular, because meat was forbidden to be served there.

The first duty of the monks on coming from the frater was to wash their hands, waiting in the cloister until all had finished their meal; then all went into the church for Nones. In summertime they went up into the dorter for their midday rest, but not in winter. When this was over, there was no service until evensong or Vespers. The brethren occupied themselves in various ways, transcribing books or reading. The novices were taught, and there was time for recreation. At Durham there was a greensward at the back of the house towards the water where the novices played bowls, the novice-master being umpire, and in winter there was often a skittle alley. On the stone seats of some cloisters are still the markings for the game of checkers. The monks were allowed to walk in the garden for exercise, and in some convents they kept strange pets; at Winchester we read of apes, peacocks and bears and other creatures being bought, not for the brethren collectively, "but by divers brethren each man for himself." This was the only time of the day when the brethren could relax from their multifarious duties and services, but with the ringing of the bell for Vespers at six o'clock, and earlier in winter, all books were replaced and they took their places in the quire.

Vespers was sung with varied ceremony according to the feast celebrated, the monks vested either in cowls, albs or copes. If not a fast-day they then went into supper in the frater, the meal consisting of one good dish and one pittance or extra dish of fruit, nuts or cheese. After supper the monks went in to church for a short time, afterwards waiting in the cloister or the chapter-house according to the season in complete silence until Collation. This consisted of a reading of no great length, after which the brethren might have a stoup of wine or beer in the frater and wait for Compline, either in the cloister, or in the winter in the common-room. The bell then rang for this last service of the day.

It will have been noted that the sound of bells was rarely absent from the air, either the small bells of the dorter, frater, chapter and church, or the greater bells of the tower. They seem to have punctuated every occasion throughout the day, and they must have given an air of animation both within and without the monastery.

The brethren then went to the dorter in procession and were not allowed to leave it until Matins. Regulations followed them even there; they were forbidden to stand upright when they were getting into bed, but were told to "sit down first upon the bed and then turn their legs under the coverlet; they were to take off their shoes under the clothes and sleep in their shirt, drawers and gaiters. No one was to sit near a light in the dorter, neither were they to sing or read there, nor must they be allowed a candle. A brother might enter the dorter during the day but ought not to linger unless he wished to change his sheets, and no strangers were to be admitted." Night did not exempt him from perpetual watchfulness. The circator took his lantern and carefully made a tour of the house. When he entered the farmery, if the inmates were in bed, he stood in the centre of the room and flashed his light round in a circle so that nothing might escape his notice. He then passed through the dorter, going down the aisle flashing his light on each side of him for the same purpose. When his examination was ended he extinguished his lantern and retired for the night.

THE SUNDAY PROCESSION

After the blessing of the water before the high altar, two priests with two brethren proceeded to take holy water round the buildings. One pair went through all the rooms surrounding the cloister sprinkling them and saying appropriate prayers; the other two went to the dorter, doing the same to each bed in turn, returning through the farmery and sprinkling the sick and infirm. Meanwhile the Sunday procession passed through the quire parclose door on the furthest side from the cloister, entering the transept and sprinkling each altar

76 DUNSTABLE PRIORY, BEDFORDSHIRE (*Augustinian*):
the Wooden Rood-screen

77 ST. ALBAN'S ABBEY, HERTFORDSHIRE (*Benedictine*):
the Stone Rood-screen

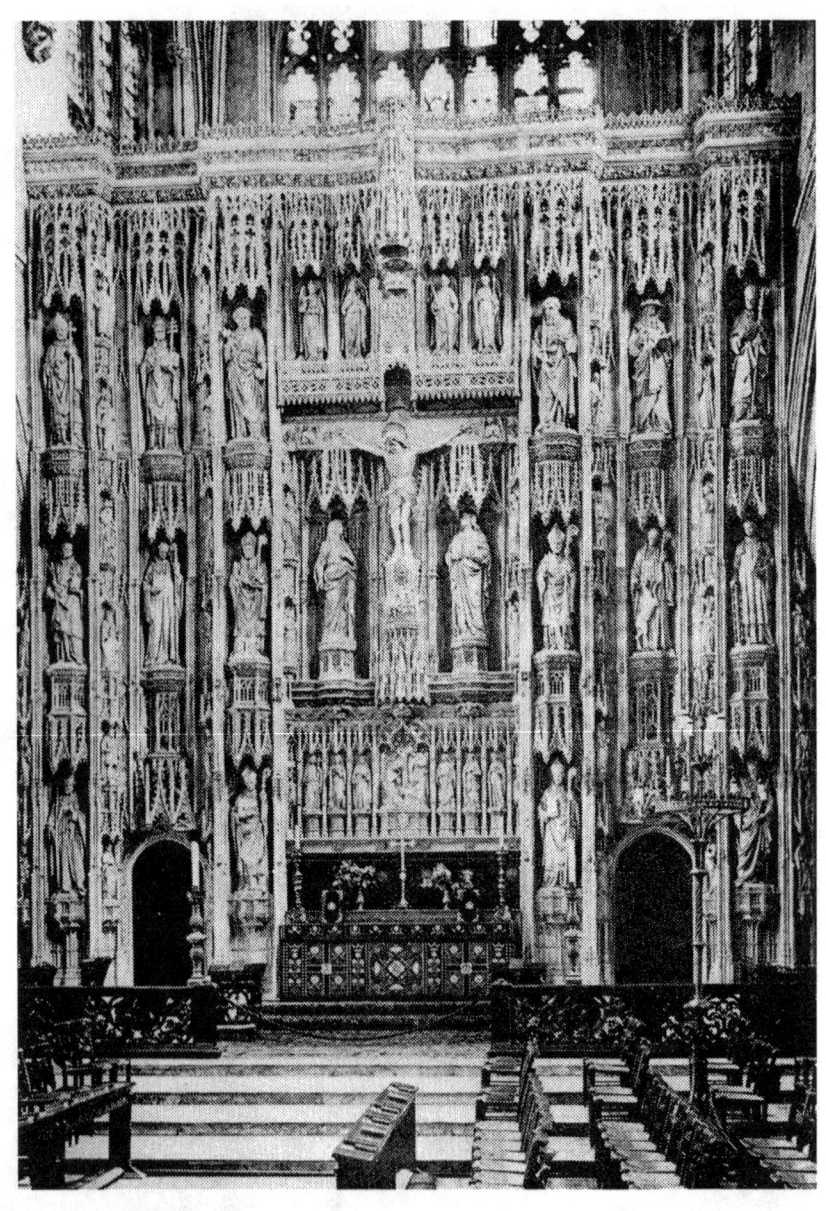

78 WINCHESTER CATHEDRAL ABBEY (*Benedictine*): the great Reredos Screen. The figures are modern

while the brethren sang an anthem. It returned by the path round the east end, and down the quire aisle into the transept nearest the cloister, sprinkling every altar, and then passed through the eastern doorway into the cloister. First walked the bearer of the holy water, next the cross-bearer between two acolytes carrying lighted candles, followed by the sub-deacon carrying the gospels in front of the priest who was to celebrate mass. The convent with the juniors at its head followed at a slow pace; the abbot, turning neither to the left nor the right, walking in the centre of the path and being the last in the procession. Each pair of brethren moved evenly and regularly four feet from the pair in front, all singing the responses. Ordinarily the procession passed once round the cloister, re-entering the church by the western processional doorway, and if there were any chapels at the west end the altars were taken in turn, the procession re-forming and proceeding up the central aisle, making its final station on the stones set for the purpose in the pavement. The nave altar was then sprinkled and those of the surrounding chapels, the procession passing through the two doorways in the rood-screen, reuniting in the bay beyond and entering the quire through the door in the pulpitum.

On Easter Day, Ascension Day, Pentecost and the Assumption of the Blessed Virgin Mary processions of great pomp took place, including the carrying of the shrine and relics, with banners and lights, all the brethren dressed in copes, the minister in tunicle and dalmatic, the vergers carrying their maces. The route included a station in the cemetery. On Palm Sunday on its return it found the west door of the church fast shut; during the singing of the *Gloria Laus*, the doors were thrown open and it entered the church making a station before the great Rood and as the bells rang out passed into the quire.

As will be noticed, the daily life of the monk was minutely directed, one day differing but little from another except for the special services and processions, and the variation between a fast day with only one meal, an ordinary day with two, and a feast day with extra allowances. Nearly every movement even of his body was regulated, and the least infringement of the endless ordinances and injunctions might be reported and punished. This continued from the day he was professed until he died or became too infirm to carry them out. All this must have led to a gradual numbing of the senses and a dulling of all those activities which make an intelligent mind. There were of course many exceptions, and the chance to rise to a position of responsibility must have been an incentive. Perhaps this was one of the reasons why so numerous a staff of officials was connected with a convent; but I am thinking more of the ordinary brother who shirked responsibility, and like a soldier was not expected to think for himself, his needs being provided for by a paternal government. There was a cause, therefore, for the various quarrels and bickerings over trifles which were magnified by the intimacy of isolation. But it is always the worst side which comes uppermost in the rolls and legal documents, whereas the peaceable and law-abiding do not appear. If present-day England was judged by the proceedings of the criminal courts, it would not come out too well. This is the point which some of our modern historians seem to overlook when they insist so much upon the value of documentary evidence.

TILE PAVING IN THE SOUTH TRANSEPT, BYLAND ABBEY

79 ST. ALBAN'S ABBEY, HERTFORDSHIRE (*Benedictine*):
Abbot Thomas Ramryge's Chapel (1540)

80 FURNESS ABBEY, LANCASHIRE (*Cistercian*):
Sedilia in the Quire

81 ST. MARK'S HOSPITAL, KNOWN AS JOHN
OF GAUNT'S, BRISTOL: Tomb of Abbot Salley (1516)

CHAPTER V

ADMINISTRATION

For the management and financing of a great monastery specially trained men were required. Unfortunately selection was limited to the inmates, and few of these had either the capacity to administer funds on a large scale, or sufficient experience to govern a community of their fellow-men. It is not surprising therefore to find that many houses were mismanaged and deeply in debt, for the Head had the power to do what seemed good in his own eyes. It was only when things became a hopeless tangle that interference came from without, either through the bishop, patron, king, or the chapter of the Order.

In the earlier days finance was a simple matter, for the lands were cultivated by conversi, villeins and serfs, and the wages were small. Later, when the properties were leased out, and servants had to be paid, the food bought (to which luxuries were added), finance became both complicated and involved. The revenues of the monasteries were never audited as a whole, for endowments and properties given for specific objects were apportioned to various obedientiaries, who thereby came to possess funds of their own; in certain cases the abbot also had his own revenue, as at Bury. An incompetent obedientiary could fritter away his income, or the abbot mortgage the estates, incurring debts far in excess of the annual revenues of the house. Although it is common to find houses deeply indebted, it is shown in the chronicles that under a wise abbot, such as Sampson of Bury, a house could be freed from debt in a dozen years. An indebted house seemed to have had a fatal facility for borrowing money from Jews and Italian financiers, and was invariably defrauded. When the appropriation of another church was sought, the reason always assigned was the poverty of the house.

Mismanagement was not the only cause for indebtedness; the abuse of hospitality, especially by the nobles, officials and royalty, contributed to its cause. The successive taxes and loans imposed by the Pope and his legate, as well as the king's constant demands for supplies for his wars and expeditions, —all these being special contributions in addition to the ordinary dues imposed on the realm in general—lessened the capacity of a monastery to continue solvent. Should the king's assent be required to the appointment of a new Head, it was given only for a consideration in money. When a monastery was exempt from the bishop's jurisdiction, the Pope and Roman Curia compelled the prospective candidate to travel to Rome, and he was there kept waiting for the confirmation of his appointment, and exorbitant charges were common. Building projects were also costly, and when carried out involved constant repair, for the buildings connected with a large monastery were more extensive than those of a modern college. The downfall of insecurely built towers, and the much-dreaded devastating fires were also a constant menace, and in the rebuilding attempts were made to keep abreast of the changing fashions in architecture; did the funds prove inadequate for entire reconstruction, the earlier walls were re-faced in the newest style, as the nave of Winchester and the quire of Gloucester. The extensive planning of the first enthusiasm generally proved altogether too large for later requirements, and the monasteries found the buildings difficult to complete, as at Selby, and later at Westminster. Bath Abbey when rebuilt was contained within the dimensions of the quire of the original church.

Monastic finance, like everything connected with the system, was traditional and of slow growth, and it was found impossible to alter it radically, although official visitors made the attempt on more than one occasion. The system of accounts varied a little in different houses of the same Order, but remained the same in essentials. The revenues of the obedientiaries came to be almost personal, and quite independent of the general fund. At times they might transfer money from one fund to another as a help in time of stress, but they looked askance at any attempt at interference or amalgamation. In their endeavours to bring the finances of the monasteries into something approaching order, the visitors introduced a new official named the bursar, through whose hands they intended that the whole of the revenues should pass. But in the end the bursar became an additional officer who looked after such revenues as were not already appropriated to specified objects. A reason for the division of the funds was the attempt to keep some slight hold upon the abbot, on whose character so much depended. His position was unassailable, and although he was not supposed to interfere with the property without

82 THE WATCHING CHAMBER AND RELIQUARY ST. ALBAN'S ABBEY, HERTFORDSHIRE (*Benedictine*)

83 THE BASE OF ST. ALBAN'S SHRINE

84 WINCHESTER CATHEDRAL ABBEY, HAMPSHIRE (*Benedictine*):
the Feretory or Shrine Chapel behind the Reredos Screen

the consent of the chapter, he could always obtain his own wishes, and the convent would endure much before it would appeal for outside help. The brethren were trained to obedience and taught to reverence their Head, and it required great courage to stand in his way or try to thwart his will.

The system of a despotic Head had many advantages, but it left the house a prey to an astute and worldly man, who was sometimes imposed from without; or it might be a victim of an incompetent inmate who, though spiritually minded, was weak, and worried by his relatives for positions and doles. An abbot like Sampson of Bury could rule with strictness, re-model his convent, replace inefficient officers, and fight the outside battles of the monastery, bringing abundance and health to the house; while Norreys of Evesham could lay the place waste and ruinous. But in neither case could the officers of the convent prevent the abbot from doing what he willed.

In 1375 the Abbot of Abingdon owed the convent £1,374, which by the end of the following year was increased by another £94. The whole amount had to be written off. In 1392 the Abbot of St. Albans borrowed £900 from the Bishop of Lichfield, which the convent had to find. In 1341 the Abbot of Lesnes was deposed by the bishop, who "judged him to be disobedient, rebellious and incorrigible, wasting the goods of the convent to the extent that the canons had not vestments to put on." The results of his extravagance fell upon his successor, for in 1354 a debt of £500 was due to the mayor of London, and the following year liabilities for £545 were admitted, both sums being twice the revenue of the house. The priory of Worcester had a heavy growing debt, and ready money had to be found by borrowing, selling crops in advance and corrodies. In the *Liber Albus* there is a memorandum for the year 1205 of a debt of £304 to Richard de la Lynde, who was later given the painted chamber in the priory and a corrody in lieu of payment. In 1371 at the Augustinian priory of Bristol, "it was found that owing to lack of good governance and neglect, the abbot has brought it low, by sale of corrodies, by hurtful demises to farm of the possessions bringing little or no profit, by waste, sale and destruction of the said possessions, excessive and fruitless expenses on manors, lands, rents, that alms and piety are withdrawn, and it is to be feared that the canons will be dispersed through lack of sustenance." Another cause of insolvency was dissension between the abbot and his convent. During the reign of Edward III in

23 out of 36 monasteries applying for relief, this was stated to be the cause, and the houses were "so loaded with debt that divine service will cease and the monks be dispersed unless a speedy remedy is applied."

It was difficult to depose an abbot. It could be done either by the visiting bishop, the head of the Order or the Pope. But this was often only the beginning of the trouble, for the deposed abbot could fight his claim from court to court and litigation was always costly. Should he win, as he sometimes did, life in the convent became more than uncomfortable. Even if unsuccessful, he might take reprisals, as at Lilleshall in 1331, and at Bindon a little earlier, when the deposed abbot attacked the house and carried away its property, or took possession of it with an armed force.

The procedure taken for helping an indebted house was as follows. Sometimes an appeal was made to the king for protection, especially against the abuse of hospitality. A clause in the first statute of Westminster decreed that none save the patron should be entertained except by invitation. This was directed against the custom whereby powerful persons with their retinues demanded hospitality and stayed for long periods; unfortunately this decree was largely ignored. In 1277 the king's steward was appointed to Flaxley abbey on account of the monastery's immense debts, "and no sheriff or other minister is to be lodged or intermeddle therein without a special licence." In 1331 the Black Prince informed the justices "that the abbeys of Chester, Combermere, and Vale Royal, all in the county, are so excessively burdened by frequent visits of people of the county with their grooms, horses and greyhounds, that their possessions hardly suffice for the maintenance of the monks." The bishop's officials were also offenders, for when consistory courts were held in adjacent towns, they lodged themselves in a neighbouring monastery for three, four, and even eight days in spite of the protests of the religious, the archbishop finding it necessary, in 1301, to prohibit such proceedings.

The men who were given the custody of an abbey and had charge of its revenues were generally laymen of good social standing. They were often friends of the convent and important landowners in the same county, and they were supposed to give personal attention to the affairs of the distressed house. They seem to have been selected in view of the particular needs of the case, such as lawyers, knights, and, if near the sea, military men, who by their position would give authority to the commission. The king's protection prevented proceedings being taken against them for immediate payment of debts, and they were granted, either temporarily or permanently the revocation of corrodies and leases detrimental to the interests of the house. It was the duty of the custodians to see that a proper number of monks was maintained, that alms and donations were properly administered, "else the souls of the donors be imperilled." Expenses in servants and food were to be reduced, and the state kept by the abbot and prior brought down to a reasonable level. If necessary, the abbot was to retire for the time being to one of the smaller establishments belonging to the abbey, all surplus funds being used for paying off the convent's debts.

The sources from which the monasteries derived their revenues are too numerous to describe in detail, but they may be divided into two, spiritualities and temporalities. The first embraced patronage, appropriated churches, pensions, and oblations at the shrines and on the altars of the church, the second all other sources of income. The oblations given at the shrines varied according to the popularity of the saint, the populace being influenced by the degree in which the person had been a rebel. St. Thomas of Canterbury combined all the necessary qualities and remained until the Reformation the most popular saint in the English calendar. Canonisation was not always necessary, for Archbishop Scrope of York also appealed to the popular imagination. He was foully murdered by Henry IV, who was excommunicated for the deed, but later Henry made his peace with the Pope, and the canonisation never took place. Nevertheless, the populace made a saint of him, and his shrine at York became one of the holiest spots in the North. It was visited by crowds of pilgrims, whose yearly offerings enabled the canons to complete the quire of their church. At Gloucester the popularity of the body of Edward II, who was murdered at the instigation of a king, enabled the monks to rebuild their quire as a glorious chantry to his honour.

It was desirable therefore for every monastery and cathedral to possess a saint, a hero, or wonder-working relic for the financial benefit of the church, such as the Holy Blood at Hailes, or the speaking crucifix at Meaux. The faithful, however, were fickle and, as in all mass movements, turned from one thing to another. During the fifteenth century oblations at shrines diminished, and by the sixteenth had become a mere trickle where they had not actually ceased.

Appropriated churches were the main revenue in spiritualities. The monks having taken the vow of poverty, represented the poor, and the great tythes, being the alms due for distribution, went into their coffers. When a church was appropriated the abbot or bishop was supposed to provide a permanent vicar at the reasonable salary of six marks a year, but this was seldom done. The whole system was wrong and led to the gravest abuse. Parliament endeavoured on several occasions to amend it, but with little result. A petition in 1432 stated, "that old men and women have died without confession or any of the sacraments of the dead, the children have died unbaptised because vicarages were left void for several years for the sake of gain."

In 1391 the priory of Lewes appropriated four churches and a chapel; thirty-five years later the parishioners complained "that the buildings had fallen into ruin, divine service was neglected, and hospitality withdrawn." The appropriation of a church included the fees for the sacraments; baptism, marriage, churching and burial. The last included according to custom the "seising" of the best horse, cow, silver and other goods belonging to the dead man. Pershore compelled the parishioners of their appropriated churches to bring their dead to the abbey. There the mortuary was valued, half going to the abbey, the other to the church. The body was then carried to the parish church where mass was said, the oblations going to the vicar. Afterwards the body was buried in the abbey churchyard, the fees going to the abbey. An instance cited by Snape from which I quote seems incredible. In 1396 the convent of Abingdon appealed as to their right to force the parishioners of St. Helens, Abingdon, to be buried in the cemetery of the monastic church; to take and exact legacies and bequests made to them on burial, and all oblations and emoluments arising from obits and anniversaries. The vicar and his parishioners had bought and consecrated a burial ground near their own church, and when the appeal was heard some sixty interments had already been made. The monastery won their suit and caused all the bodies to be exhumed, and the vicar and his parishioners were obliged to pay the costs of the suit and of the removal of the bodies to the abbey ground.

Patronage should not have meant any emoluments to the

85 WESTMINSTER ABBEY, LONDON (*Benedictine*): the North Cloister Alley

86 GREY FRIARS, COVENTRY: North Cloister Walk, now used as the Poor House

87 NEWMINSTER ABBEY, NORTHUMBERLAND (*Cistercian*): re-erected portion of Cloister Wall

abbeys, but the constant changing of vicars every three or four years, especially in some districts, gives a bad impression. Archbishop Peckham, speaking of the priory of Lewes in 1285, said, "They should take care to present to the cure of souls men who by example and word may show themselves shepherds, not robbers. We have passed the flower of youth, and already are attaining to old age, and on careful retrospection, we can hardly remember that to the present day we ever saw a man presented by the prior to the cure of souls in the sincerity which is needful."

Temporalities included all other sources of income: lands given by the patrons and others in various parts of the country, manorial rights and dues which were often extorted to the last penny; farming profits, with income from pools, woods and pastures; leases, tenant services and the work of villeins and serfs; mills and wharfage; judicial courts with their fees, wardships, homages and all the paraphernalia of medieval, and for that matter of modern customs used for the extracting of money from people.

There were also revenues from the towns which had grown up under the protection of the monasteries, including tenements, and the granting of fairs and markets either by the patron or the king. These proved profitable in tolls. At Westminster, Henry III wishing to supplement the money for building the quire, gave the convent a fair for a fortnight, and compelled all the citizens of London to close their shops and trade there, much to their indignation. At Chester, the abbey had a fair granted to them by Hugh Lupus, to be held outside the abbey gateway, including the right to set up booths and rent them out. Traders were forbidden for its duration to sell or buy within five miles of the city other than at the fair. At Bury the London merchants claimed exemption, and not obtaining it kept away for two years, "to the detriment of the fair, and the loss of the sacrist." Dover had the right to three fairs a year, passage dues, tolls on the Saturday market, and a tenth of the herring fishery, with a toll of the sea and wreckage. As the towns grew in size the convents were compelled to meet the citizens half-way, and levied dues in place of tolls, thereby freeing the trade in the towns.

Fisheries, owing to the monks' diet, were important, and nearly every abbey had its fishing rights. Chester had a free boat on the Dee, fishing rights off Anglesea for a ship and ten nets, and the tythes of some of the best fisheries in the country. Vale Royal let their weirs at Warford on the Weaver for forty-eight strikes of eels and twelve large eels annually. All rivers had to have the centre of the stream clear of nets; at Chester it was to be wide enough for a boat twenty-five feet broad with oars sixteen feet long.

Monasteries were also trading communities. Durham had coalmines at Ferryhill and Gateshead, with the right of timber for the pits and water-gate. Finchale had a coalmine in 1486 with a pumping station worked by a horse. In the twelfth century St. Bees, and Byland, mined for iron, and Kirkstead had four forges, two for smelting and two for working iron, with the right to dig for ore and to take dead wood for fuel. Bolton priory had lead mines, and many houses owned salt-pits, including Birkenhead, Chester, Combermere, Stanlaw and Vale Royal in Cheshire; Lilleshall, Shrewsbury and Wenlock in Salop; Burton, Dieulacres and Ronton in Staffordshire; and Basingwerk in Flint. In 1306 Vale Royal held Northwich in ferm for £76. When a fire occurred which destroyed sixty-five salt-pits, the abbot was allowed £25 in recompense for his losses. In 1284 the Abbot of Vale Royal was allowed to take ferm in Mottram Forest for glass-making. In 1309 he complained that whereas Edward I had granted a quarry in the Forest of Delamere with other easements for the making of glass, he was now prevented from rebuilding the house used by his predecessors. Monasteries had other trades in their hands. St. Albans had a fulling mill, and compelled all the weavers in the town to use it. Meaux had a tannery where they kept a store of "cow and calf leather, sole peces, sclepe, chowthedys and wambes to the value of £14 10s. 4d., together with 15 tubs and various tools and tan from the oaks barked during each year." Repton and Malvern had tile works. In 1238 Tewkesbury sold to the king's household a tun of wine made from their vineyards.

Their principal asset was however the wool staple, famous throughout Europe. Nearly all monastic houses possessed flocks of sheep, and when in difficulties often sold the wool for several years in advance. A letter in Abbot Gregory's book of Whalley abbey is worth quoting as showing the methods employed. "Whereby the abbey contracts to sell sixteen sacks of home-grown wool, without coth, gard, black, grey, putrid scab, torn-off skin, grease, clact, bard, or bad skin," for a certain sum of ready money, which the merchant would pay to their representative at Boston. The

88 TYNEMOUTH PRIORY, NORTHUMBERLAND (*Benedictine*):
Sedilia, Piscina and Aumbry in Quire

89 GLOUCESTER CATHEDRAL ABBEY (*Benedictine*):
the 12th-Century Slype

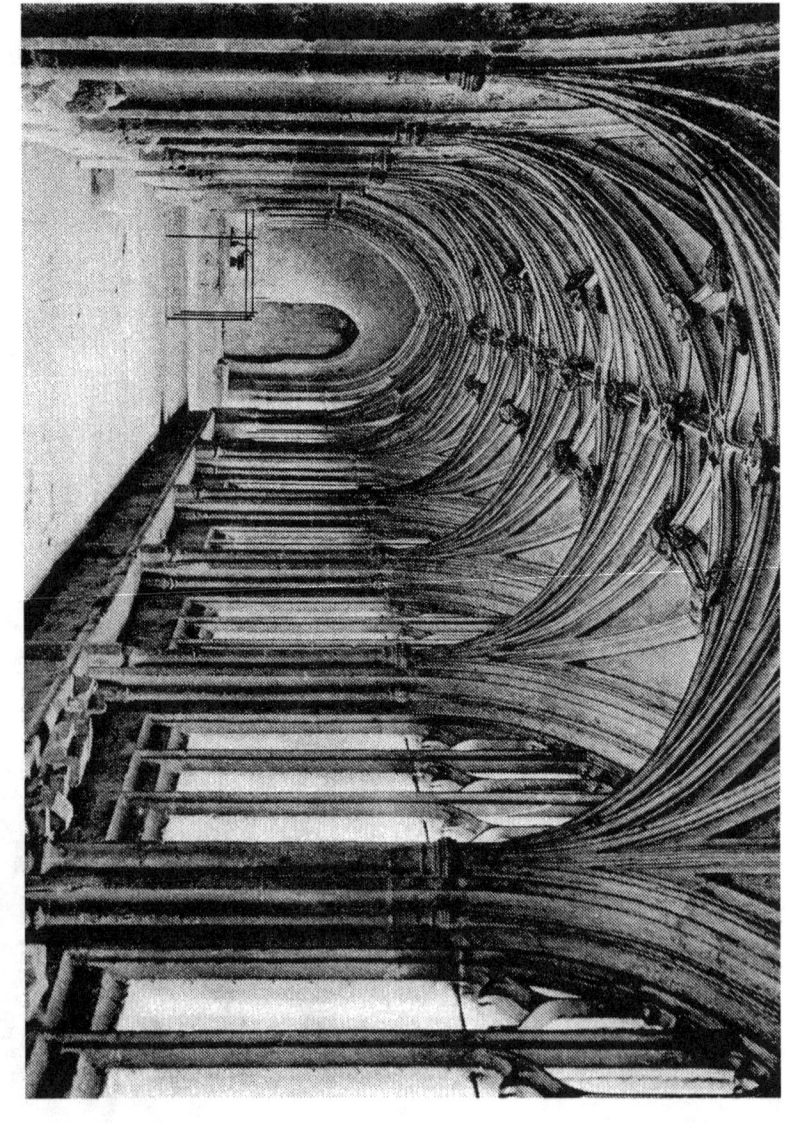

90 LACOCK ABBEY, WILTSHIRE (*Augustinian Nuns*): the Cloister South Walk

abbey undertook "to deliver the wool at their own expense and peril, well washed, dry, and free from faults, of proper weight, weighed according to the custom of the house, in two instalments, unless prevented by a war in England or violent confiscation by the king; under penalty of £10 sterling for every sack in default. If, however, the king seized the wool in the first year, the merchant was to have all the wool for three years at 6½ marks for every sack; if the king seized it the second year and not the first, then he was to have the wool for one year at the same rate." At Dover in 1490, a special licence was granted to the prior and John Fox, merchant of London, to export from London, Southampton, Sandwich, or one of them, to foreign parts beyond the straits of Gibraltar, thirty sacks of barded and cleansed wool without paying any customs or subsidies thereon.

In addition to the ordinary expenditure there were other charges to be met: the taxation imposed by Pope and King, levies of various sorts and charges made for leave to carry on the affairs of a monastery, such as the dues for permission to elect the head of a house, or alter its financial system. With the commencement of a new reign the deeds of the abbey had to be proved, and there was continual litigation over the monastery's possessions. These various burdens often proved altogether too much for the revenues and were one of the main causes of its indebtedness. Official visitors, either the bishop or those appointed by the Orders, came at intervals to examine the administration and conduct of a house. This was a wasteful charge, for the bishop travelled in state with a large retinue, and, apart from the fees due to him, both he and his company expected to be well entertained. Archbishops were allowed to have as many as fifty horses in their train, bishops thirty, cardinals twenty-five. In addition the servants required presents. A visitation to the small house of Eynsham included £6 for the servants, including a cook, nine squires, thirteen valets, three grooms, a kitchen valet, two kitchen pages and a messenger. Moreover a bishop was an awkward person to cross. The convent at Whalley had, with the Papal permission, appropriated the parish church during the bishop's imprisonment. On his release he took away the church and fined them 1,000 marks, which they were compelled to repay at 200 marks a year. How hardly they were placed is shown by an agreement dated 1304 to deliver seventeen sacks of wool to Boston in payment of a debt of £85 advanced to them in their great necessity. Evesham in claiming exemption from the bishop's visitations said "they knew not the episcopal burdens. Not only once a year, but as often as he will, he visits the monasteries subjected to him. Not only the bishops, but even their archdeacons, officials and ministers are admitted to the great grievance of the house, and their horses are put to lodge until they are bettered by their stay there: even the rents are wont to be given to the clerks of the bishops, with other intolerable presents, all of which are to be borne at one time, and the neighbours yet more heavily." The powers of ecclesiastics are shown in a visit of Archbishop Winchelsey to Worcester in 1301, when at the close of his visitation "he deposed the sub-prior, precentor, chamberlain, sacrist, third-prior and pitancer, confining the last three within the walls of the house for a year. He found that Bishop Gifford had erected a solid and costly tomb to himself at the south end of the principal altar, which interfered with the conduct of the services, which he ordered to be taken down within eight days."

Many of the greater abbeys struggled to free themselves from episcopal control, but found in doing so that they had if anything worsened their position. When the abbot of an exempted house was elected, he was compelled to travel to Rome for confirmation, bearing not only the cost of the journey, but the many delays by the Curia. In 1257 Simon de Luton, prior, was elected Abbot of Bury, for which he paid 2,000 marks. In 1279 John of Northwold paid 1,175 marks. Henry Peckham was consecrated Archbishop of Canterbury by the Pope, for which he paid 4,000 marks, and an additional 2,000 to the king for sanctioning it. John Maryns on being elected to St. Albans paid 2,258 marks, not including his journey to the Roman Court. The next abbot of the same house, Hugh de Evresdone, spent over £1,000 in having his election confirmed. At Westminster in 1259, Richard obtained a papal faculty to contract a loan of 1,000 marks to meet his expenses incurred in Rome, and in 1320 Abbot William was relieved from excommunication by paying 8,000 florins.

The cupidity of the Roman Curia did not stay at such expedients as these. During the oppressive days of Henry III there is a record of continual exactions and extortions, both by Pope and king, who when it suited their convenience combined together. It was said they resembled the wolf

91 HAUGHMOND ABBEY, SHROPSHIRE (*Augustinian*): Entrance to Chapter-house

92 LACOCK ABBEY, WILTSHIRE (*Augustinian Nuns*):
the Chapter-house

and the shepherd together harrying the fold, each trying all kinds of inducements and expedients for extracting money from the religious. In 1229 the Pope took tythe from the clergy, which was paid under threat of excommunication. This threat was used so often and for such material ends, that its terror must have been lessened by constant use. In 1240 the heads of all religious houses were summoned to London to meet the legate Otho. They in their turn formulated complaints against the king. Churches had been kept vacant, the rights and liberties of the clerics had been ignored and abused. Promises were made to them, but the money demanded from them was not forthcoming. The legate then sent letters requiring immediate payments of large sums for the proper support of his dignity in the country, at the same time offering to excuse those who had taken a crusading oath, on payment of fines which were to go into the papal coffers. In the late spring the heads of the Church were again summoned with an instant demand for huge sums to help in the war made by the Pope against the Emperor Frederick, which were refused. The abbots could ill spare the large sums extorted from them to be sent to Rome. Bury and Battle complained to the king, who handed them over to the legate, offering at the same time to provide a fitting prison for their reception, and it was only in this extremity that the majority gave in. During 1240, as the legate had failed in his purpose in full assembly, he attacked them in smaller numbers, starting in Berkshire. They again opposed his demands and replying to him said "that just as the Roman church had its patrimony, the administration of which belonged to the Lord Pope, so the English churches had theirs, which was not liable to pay tribute to the Roman church; and if all churches were under the care and guardianship of the Pope, they were not under his dominion, nor were they his property."

Towards the end of the year the legate left for Rome, but not before he had summoned another meeting, at which he was aided by the king; and all gave way except the Cistercians. In 1254 the Pope gave the king a tenth of all ecclesiastical property, and the following year, when the legate Rustard was opposed by the clergy, he obtained letters in blank to send to any monastery he pleased. He ordered them to raise money by borrowing, either five, six, or seven hundred marks for the use of the Pope. In 1255 he summoned the Heads to London and demanded so large a sum that had it been granted, the Church and kingdom would have been ruined. At their refusal the legate and the king were angered, for both the king and the Pope were deeply involved in the foolish claim to the crown of Sicily. In 1256 the king ordered the Abbot of Westminster to pay 1,705 marks, which the king owed to merchants in Siena, and at the same time Rustard claimed five years' tax on first-fruits. The Pope also insisted on the immediate finding of 2,000 marks to pay his creditors; the Prior of Durham had to find 500 marks, Bath, Crowland and Thorney 400 each, and Guisborough 300, Rustard demanding the whole year's crop of wool from the Cistercians, which was refused.

This did not complete the conscription of the religious houses. Both Pope and king presented the best livings to foreigners, who were often absentees and took the emoluments without discharging the obligations; and when they did, their presence was more aggravating than their absence. In 1306 a papal bull conferred on John Boter a benefice with or without a cure of souls as soon as vacant, to the value of sixty marks with no deductions, now in the gift of the priory of Worcester. "His deficiency in orders and age do not bar this, and we give him a dispensation." John Boter was a foreigner aged twelve. The see of Winchester becoming vacant, the king installed his half-brother as bishop. He was a youth, not even in holy orders, who could not speak English, but had already been presented to benefices whose revenues equalled that of the Archbishop of Canterbury. As was said of him, "he had not even the rudiments of learning and grammar. Ignorant of our language, of scripture, and all clerical learning, he cannot preach or hear confessions, or indeed minister to God in any spiritual office." No sooner was he installed than he fell foul of the convent and locked the monks in the church for three days, from which hardship some of the weaker brethren never recovered. A few fled to other houses, but "he filled their places with low-bred, ignorant and wholly unworthy men, and turned out the prior for a nominee of his own, acting to the scandal of the entire monastic order."

During the reign of Edward III there was little improvement. The monasteries in turn were charged with the duty of collecting the convocation grants, and shared in the unpopularity of all papal exactions. In 1331 the abbot of Burton's servant was assaulted and robbed of £100 which he had

93 BIRKENHEAD PRIORY, CHESHIRE *(Benedictine)*: the Chapter-house, now a Chapel

94 CHESTER CATHEDRAL ABBEY *(Benedictine)*: the Parlour, now Library

95 VALLE CRUCIS ABBEY, DENBIGHSHIRE (*Cistercian*) : the 14th-Century Chapter-house

96 CHESTER CATHEDRAL ABBEY (*Benedictine*) : the Chapter-house Vestibule, 13th Century

97 DURHAM CATHEDRAL ABBEY (*Benedictine*): the Dormitory, now used as a library

98 HEXHAM PRIORY, NORTHUMBERLAND (*Augustinian*):
the Night Stairs from the Dormitory. 13th Century

99 CHESTER CATHEDRAL ABBEY (*Benedictine*): the Day
Stairs to the Dormitory. 14th Century

collected for the Pope. During the king's various wars he was unremitting in his endeavours to obtain assistance both in goods, money, and daily necessaries. The *Liber Albus* of Worcester records various demands for carrying out his Scotch wars: In 1310 he commanded 60 quarters of wheat, 40 quarters of barley meal, 20 oxen and 100 sheep "to be delivered to our sheriff to be conveyed to Scotland ready for our arrival." He also demanded wagons and horses and subsidies of money for the same purpose. In 1321 he ordered as many strong fighting men as possible, well mounted and equipped, for fighting in the Welsh Marches. In reply to this last demand, the prior wrote: "Since the property in common with that of others in the realm is depressed by pestilence and death, and in particular by the men of might who have come from the Marches, and their long stays, and now worse than all this by the coming of the magnates who have lately made perquisitions in Worcester, they have left nothing in the country. Having regard to the matters aforesaid and the distress and want which they suffer in eating and drinking and other necessities they will be excused."

In 1347 the king issued a demand of money and wool, which he expected to realise £3,500, in addition to the sixteenth demanded the year before. He also tried other methods. He had twenty thousand sacks of wool sold to the farmers of the customs at 23s. 4d. under the proper price. In return the merchants were to pay the King £40,000 between April and July; £10,000 between August and September, and £16,000 between September and Christmas. Meanwhile all ports were closed, and any wool taken out of the realm was forfeit to the king.

Events recorded in the history of the times had their repercussions on the fortunes of the monasteries. The Scotch wars involved many Northern abbeys in disaster and pillage, their estates being laid waste, when the buildings were not actually destroyed. The Pestilence during the fourteenth century destroyed their financial system, and they were obliged to adopt new methods as labour grew scarce. In place of farming their own lands they had to lease them out, their tenements in the towns remaining unoccupied and falling into ruin. The farm of mills was less, fisheries less, plots of land remained uncultivated, the eyre of woods was not held, mills stood in need of repair; the peasantry demanded higher wages, and dealers raised their prices, and many sources of revenue dried up. The Wars of the Roses in the fifteenth century caused the loss of many estates, the monasteries becoming involved in the political fortunes of their patrons. Tutbury in 1321 was mixed up in the revolt of Thomas of Lancaster, who on fleeing from Edward II left his war-chest behind him. The convent were accused of its possession, and harried until 1325, when they were exonerated. Five hundred years later, when workmen were clearing out the mill-race sixty yards below the bridge, they discovered hundreds of coins in gold and silver, English, Scottish and French, which at that late date cleared the monks.

There were many reasons for a state of indebtedness, as the foregoing matter indicates. The constant demands and exactions from Rome must have been intolerable; not only irritating but impoverishing the religious houses and clergy, as well as alarming the laity on account of so much money leaving the country. These, combined with the insatiable needs of improvident monarchs, must have driven the Heads of the monasteries to absolute despair.

DETAIL OF THE GATEWAY, KIRKHAM PRIORY

100 DURHAM CATHEDRAL ABBEY (*Benedictine*): the Water Conduit House

101 NORWICH CATHEDRAL ABBEY (*Benedictine*): the Lavatory

102 CANTERBURY CATHEDRAL ABBEY (*Benedictine*): the Water Tower

CHAPTER SIX

BUILDING

WITH the advent of the Normans the country was quickly organised as a building unit. Numerous monasteries and castles were being erected in the heavy, thick-walled, rough-finished manner evolved, by a few competent masons, who had to train and manage a horde of amateurs in the elements of wall construction. I suggest a "building unit," for the population of the whole country did not exceed that of present-day Yorkshire.

In the early years, members of the monasteries lent a helping hand in the erection of their future homes, as a little later the conversi of the Cistercians built their first temporary quarters; but this was soon abandoned, and the design and construction of cathedrals, monasteries and castles were placed entirely in lay hands. The assertions constantly made in the various chronicles that bishops, abbots, priors and sacrists were the architects and builders, must be qualified by the statement made by Matthew Paris in 1054, "that all works must be ascribed to the abbot out of respect to his office, for he who sanctions the performance of a thing by his authority, is really the person who does the thing." No doubt these officials had not only the ordering of the work, but gave their decision upon its size and the type of architecture desired, it often being stated that a building should be like one already erected, but better if possible. The funds passed through their hands, and the sacrist or a clerk was appointed to keep the accounts. With the actual setting out and construction, however, they had little or nothing to do. The period under review extended over four hundred years, and during that time the building system changed gradually in the direction of the work being placed in the hands of men of professional standing, free from amateur interference.

When a building was to be erected the first step taken was the appointment of a working architect, called the master-mason, who took charge of the design, construction and management of the work. This was generally a well-paid position, and included a house together with a fur coat and gloves; if the work was on a large scale it was permanent with a pension attached. Nothing better than the working architect has been devised, and it is a thousand pities for architecture that he was ever superseded by professional gentlemen often without practical experience.

The master-mason had an assistant, but he alone was responsible for the engagement of the masons and workpeople under him. Owing to the scattered nature of their employment, the masons were more or less nomadic in their habits, and seem to have had permission to travel from place to place. They moved about in small gangs, possibly owing to the perils of the road, and some of them owned horses and carts, which suggests their methods of travel. If they brought their own tools, these were bought from them when they started work and sold back when they left. When a king had important works on hand he would order the sheriffs of the different counties to impress masons under pain of fine and imprisonment; this was done for the building of the royal castles and houses. Owing to the nature of their work masons do not seem to have had gilds of their own in the towns, although they did join other gilds; they had however ordinances largely of municipal origin, but were not organised in the strict way that other craftsmen were.

There were various grades of masons who were paid according to their ability. The highest class were the freemasons, who worked the fine-grained freestones with chisel and mallet, and cut the tracery, moulded the arches and caps and executed the carving. There were also rough-masons, wallers, layers, and paviors; scapplers shaped the stones with hammers instead of axes and generally worked in the quarries. The carpenters were gild men, as their occupation was a settled one, the majority of the villages being built of timber and clay. They were required for making templets for the masons, building lodges for the workmen, erecting scaffolds as well as roofing. The diggers and carters were also local men.

The erection of a monastery was no light undertaking. Apart from the church, there were numerous adjacent buildings, together with the drainage, water-supply, fishponds, enclosing walls and gates. It was beyond the capacity of any one house to provide funds for the whole work to be carried through without a break, unless the monastery was a small one. Three examples of building on a large scale are here given from existing chronicles and fabric rolls. The first is an eye-witness account of the fire which consumed the quire at

103 FOUNTAINS ABBEY, YORKSHIRE (*Cistercian*): the 13th-Century Refectory, once divided by a row of pillars

104 RIEVAULX ABBEY, YORKSHIRE (*Cistercian*): the 13th-Century Refectory, built on an undercroft owing to the fall of the land

105 GLOUCESTER CATHEDRAL ABBEY (*Benedictine*): the 15th-Century Cloister Lavatory

Canterbury in 1174; the second notes the rebuilding of the quire at Westminster by Henry III (1245-1270); the third

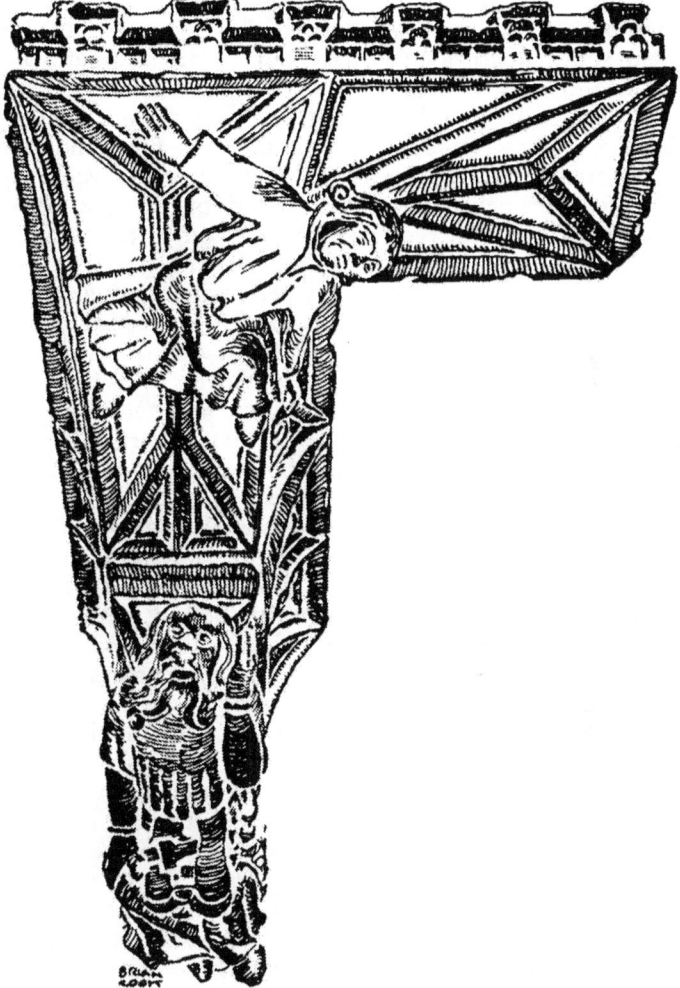

MONUMENT TO A MASON'S APPRENTICE WHO FELL FROM THE TOWER DURING BUILDING, GLOUCESTER

tells of the foundation of Vale Royal by Edward I (1278-1280).

The graphic account in the tract by Gervase the monk "On

the burning and repair of the Church at Canterbury," printed by Willis in 1845, remains our earliest and best description of building activity in the twelfth century. It took place at 3 p.m. on September 5, 1174. "In the aforesaid year on the nones of September, at the ninth hour, and during an extraordinary violent south wind, a fire broke out before the gate of the church, and outside the walls of the monastery, by which three cottages were half destroyed. From thence, while the citizens were assembling and subduing the fire, cinders and sparks carried aloft by the high wind, were deposited upon the church, and being driven by the fury of the wind between the joints of the lead, remained there amongst the half-rotten planks, and shortly glowing with increasing heat, set fire to the rotten rafters; no one as yet perceiving or helping. For the well-painted ceiling below, and the sheet-lead covering above, concealed between them the fire that had arisen within. The popular excitement having subsided, everybody went home again, while the neglected church was consuming with internal fire unknown to all. But beams and braces burning, the flames rose to the slopes of the roof; and the sheets of lead yielding to the increasing heat began to melt. The raging wind, finding freer entrance, increased the fury of the fire; and the flames beginning to show themselves, a cry arose: See! see! the church is on fire. And now that the fire had loosened the beams from the pegs that bound them together, the half-burnt timbers fell into the quire below upon the seats of the monks; the seats consisting of a great mass of woodwork, caught fire, and thus the mischief grew worse and worse, for the flames multiplied by this mass of timber, and extending upwards twenty-five feet, scorched and burnt the walls, more especially the columns of the church. In this manner the house of God, hitherto delightful as a paradise of pleasures, was now made a despicable heap of ashes, reduced to a dreary wilderness, and laid open to all the injuries of the weather. The people were astonished that the Almighty should suffer such things, and maddened with excess of grief and perplexity, they tore their hair and beat the walls and pavement with their heads and hands, blaspheming the Lord and his saints, the patrons of the church; and many, both of laity and monks, would rather have laid down their lives than that the church should be so miserably perished.

"Bethink what mighty grief oppressed the hearts of the sons of the church under this tribulation; truly that they

106 CLEEVE ABBEY, SOMERSET (*Cistercian*): the Refectory, rebuilt on an Undercroft in the 15th Century

107 THE INTERIOR OF THE ABOVE, LOOKING EAST.
Note the Remains of the painted Rood on the East Wall

108 BEAULIEU ABBEY, HAMPSHIRE (*Cistercian*) : Refectory Pulpit.
The Building is now used as a Church. 13th Century

might alleviate their miseries with a little consolation, they put together as well as they could, an altar and station in the nave, where they might wail rather than sing their services, and so the brethren remained in grief and sorrow for five years, separated from the people only by a low wall. Meanwhile the brethren sought counsel as to how the burnt church might be repaired, but without success; for the pillars were weakened by the heat and were scaling in places, so that they frightened even the wisest out of their wits. French and English artificers were summoned, but these differed in opinion. Some said they could repair the pillars without mischief to the walls above, others that the whole church must be pulled down. However, amongst them was a certain William of Sens, a Man active and ready, and as a workman most skilful both in wood and stone. Him therefore they retained, on account of his lively genius and good reputation and dismissed the others. And he residing many days with the monks carefully surveyed the walls, yet did for some time conceal the truth from them for fear it would kill them. But he went on preparing all things needful for the work and when the monks were somewhat comforted ventured to tell them the truth and at length they agreed to the total destruction of the quire. He then procured stone from beyond the sea, constructing ingenious machines for loading and unloading ships and drawing cement and stones. He made moulds for shaping the stones to the sculptors assembled, and diligently prepared other things of the same kind, and the quire was pulled down and nothing else done that year."

Gervase then describes in detail the progress of the work during the next three years, which may be omitted. Taking up the thread at the fourth year we find that "in the summer, commencing from the cross, he erected ten pillars, being five on each side. Upon these he placed the arches and vaults. And having completed both sides of the triforia and clerestories, was at the beginning of the fifth year in the act of preparing with machines for the turning of the great vault, when suddenly the beams broke under his feet, and he fell to the ground, stones and timbers accompanying his fall from the upper vault, say fifty feet. Thus sorely bruised by the blows from the beams and stones, he was rendered helpless alike to himself and for his work, but no other person than himself was in the least injured. Against the master only was this vengeance of God or spite of the devil directed. The master thus hurt remained in his bed under medical care in expectation of recovering, but was deceived. Nevertheless, as the winter approached, he gave charge of the work to a certain ingenious and industrious monk who was overseer of the masons; an appointment whence much envy and malice arose, because it made this young man appear more skilful than richer and more powerful ones. But the master reclining in bed commanded all things that should be done in order. In these operations the fourth year was occupied and the beginning of the fifth. And the master perceiving that he derived no benefit from the physicians, gave up his work, and crossing the sea, returned to his home in France. And another succeeded him in the charge of the works, William by name, English by nation, small in body, but in workmanship acute and honest." Gervase then continues his narrative until the tenth year.

Two or three points in the foregoing are worth consideration. In the twelfth century working architects were employed to design and construct buildings connected with monasteries. They were selected by competition, chosen for their capacity for a special undertaking. Only one monk is mentioned as having anything to do with the construction, and he is spoken of as the overseer of the masons. If we read between the lines, we visualise the ingenious young monk as being none other than Gervase himself, who as clerk of the works followed it closely from its inception, and was called upon by William of Sens in his extremity to carry out his instructions. I think we should be safe in surmising that the funds for this undertaking were provided by the offerings at the shrine of St. Thomas à Becket.

The second work to be noticed is the rebuilding of the eastern half of Westminster Abbey by Henry III (1245–1269). The King was a determined, headstrong monarch with a passion for building and for the collection of art treasures; St. Edward the Confessor being his patron saint, he from the first lavished gifts on his shrine and church, and willed his body to be buried beside that of his patron. It is therefore not surprising that he conceived the idea of a church comparable with the great French buildings such as Rheims, Amiens, Beauvais and the Sainte Chapelle in Paris, which were arising before his eyes. He made preparations the year before the actual start of the work by ordering the sheriff of Kent to provide a hundred barges for the conveyance of stone, and that all stone for London should be diverted to Westminster; also that all persons having grey stone for sale should take it to the abbey. The Confessor's church had first to be demolished, upon which a start was made on July 6, 1245. There was no question as to lack of funds so long as the King was kept in a good humour. He appointed his master-mason, his master-carpenter, and his clerk of works, Edward of Westminster. The master-mason was Henry of Reynes, from either Rheims or Reynes in Essex; Reynes dying in 1253, John of Gloucester succeeded him, who in turn gave place to Robert of Beverley, all of them being the King's master-masons who looked after the royal palaces and castles, in addition to the work at Westminster Abbey. The eager and impatient monarch expended money at the rate of £2,000 a year, and from time to time issued orders for the expedition of the work, as in 1250 when he commanded that at least six to eight hundred men should be at work on the building. The dedication of the new building took place on October 13, 1269, after twenty-five years of labour at a cost of £50,000. Here as at Canterbury there is no mention of monks, with the single exception of the King's beloved painter, Master William of Winchester.

Our third example is concerned with the foundation and erection of a large convent remote from either town or village. Again we have a royal foundation and the fabric rolls for the first three years have been preserved. Edward I, owing to a threatened shipwreck, vowed to found a monastery to the glory of God, and he turned for help to the Cistercian Abbey Dore in Herefordshire, whose monks had shown him former kindness. A nucleus left Dore for Darnhall in Cheshire, which after a time proving unsuitable, they chose another site near the River Weaver in the Vale Royal of England. In 1277 the foundation-stones were laid with great pomp by the King and his Consort. He had set apart monies for the work from his Palatinate of Cheshire, and appointed Leonius his collector to manage the financial side. The fabric rolls for the three years he was in charge are full of interesting details. The master-mason was Walter of Hereford, who had also charge of several other royal buildings. He received in wages two shillings a day; his assistant John of Battle three shillings a week, other masons being paid from half-a-crown downwards. The total number of masons employed during this time was 131, and they came from all quarters of England; their average stay being but for a few months, when they moved on to another lodge. Their names suggest the places of their origin; only seven came from cities and towns, the others from country districts or the neighbourhood of abbeys where building construction was being carried out on a large scale, such as Buildwas, Dore, Eynsham, Flaxley, Furness, Leominster, Norton, Pershore, Roche, St. Albans, Thurgarton and Winchcombe, or from villages containing large churches such as Checkley, Marcle, Melbourne and Tong. Very few local names appear on the lists.

During these early years the time was spent upon foundations and walls, fine masonry for windows and arches being in a tentative state. Nevertheless, the quantity of stone quarried and brought to the site was extraordinary. The quarries were four miles distant, and during the period under review 35,448 loads of stone were carried. In addition to the masons, carpenters and carters, large gangs of diggers, quarrymen and smiths were employed. The cost to the king amounted to £1,000 a year, and his total outlay is said to have been over £32,000. The monks left Darnhall in 1281 for a small temporary building, evidently constructed of timber near the new site, as the carpenters were busily engaged erecting lodges for the workmen and the monks. They cut out of the Forest of Delamere 12,800 boards, for which 67,000 nails were provided. Laths and clay were also used. During the three recorded years there is no mention of either monks or laymen having any connection with the work, and the account does not supply the picture of monks busily engaged on the construction of their own dwellings. They did not enter into their new home until 1330, and the buildings were still far from complete. They continued, however, to receive royal help, the Black Prince in 1353 giving a grant of 500 marks and supplementing it with another 500 in 1358. New steps were taken to complete the work in 1359, when the Prince and the abbot on the one part, and Master William de Helpston, the king's mason, on the other part, undertook to make twelve chapels round the quire of the church, this contract being the first we find connected with Vale Royal in which direct labour was not employed.

In none of the above undertakings was there any lack of funds, but this was exceptional; if a monastery was unable to rely upon monies given to a popular saint or hero as at Canterbury, Gloucester, Hayles or York, or by benevolent

109 SHREWSBURY ABBEY (*Benedictine*) : Refectory Pulpit. The rest of the Building has been destroyed. The Abbey Church Tower is in the background

110 GLASTONBURY ABBEY, SOMERSET (*Benedictine*): the Abbey Kitchen, with St. Joseph's Chapel beyond

patrons, were they kings, bishops or abbots, but had to fall back upon its own limited resources, it became a hopeless struggle, and at times even the necessary repairs remained undone. An important monastery with royal patrons, such as Westminster, found it impossible to carry out projected schemes without energetic backing from outside, as the endeavour to complete the nave of the church sufficiently shows. After the completion of the eastern half by Henry III, the Confessor's nave remained for over a hundred years, a lower building butting up against the new work. In 1375 Cardinal Langham provided funds to proceed with a new nave, but, as Abbot Lithyngton said, it would be easier to build a new church on a new site than pull down the existing nave. It took twelve years to demolish, and was not completely cleared away until 1376. From that date until the suppression it was a-building nearly two hundred years, and remained incomplete when the abbey was dissolved. The master-masons during this long period included Henry Yevele, who must be given the credit of the design; William of Colchester, John of Thirsk, John of Reading and Robert Stowell. It is interesting to observe how many of the master-masons mentioned in these various accounts were from the country.

There are many points of interest connected with the actual building of monasteries which should be noted. At Vale Royal the stone for the abbey was conveyed in carts, there being no suitable waterways or rivers, but in the wilds of Yorkshire, during the middle of the twelfth century, the abbey of Rievaulx, under Abbot Ailred, constructed waterways to convey their stone to the building. They made rough sledge roads down the hill-sides to the valley to dams or small harbours, and from thence cut canals to the site, using the water from the small River Rye to float their stone. They had more than one quarry, the first up the valley, of soft stone, used in their Norman building; later a finer stone from down the valley used for the rebuilding, to which the canals were extended. They also quarried ironstone and had a forge, the canals providing the carriage.

Apart from the churches, large numbers of monastic buildings were first constructed of timber, and it was a long process converting them into stone, which may account for the numerous fires which are recorded. When stone was used for walls, the roofs remained in timber, the exterior covering being often of the same material or thatch. At Croxden as late as 1332, the general re-roofing was made with shingles, the cloisters taking, according to the computation of the carpenter, 25,000. Later in the year the frater and its belfry took 19,000, "so that those who came after might devote themselves in greater peace to divine worship"; two years later 30,000 shingles were used for the dorter, rere-dorter and abbot's lodging. At Bury in 1150 the conventual buildings were destroyed by fire, including the refectory, dorter, chapter-house, infirmary and abbot's lodging; during a riot in 1327 they were again burnt, the loss being assessed at £140,000, and in 1465 the church was gutted. In 1298 a fire at Westminster destroyed the frater, dorter, infirmary and abbot's hall, and the list could be extended indefinitely.

In their planning and construction the monasteries were in advance of their time, and they were also the pioneers of water-supply and drainage. At Canterbury as early as the twelfth century there was a complete water-supply conveyed through lead pipes, of which the plan has been preserved in the library of Trinity College, Cambridge. The source was outside the north wall of the city, and the water was first taken to a tower (102), then passing under the city walls it fed the lavatories, cisterns, bath-house, kitchens and fish-ponds of the convent. Before coming into the city it passed through five filter beds, so constructed as to be easily cleaned out. At various places it could be drawn off by means of stop-cocks; in the people's cemetery, there was a pedestal fixed to enable it to be taken by dipping in a pail; and at the conduit-house a column to give a head pressure to the water. At Chester in 1285 the water for the convent was conveyed three miles from Christleton, where a tank twenty feet square was constructed, with another in the cloister, a pipe being laid between the two; the king granted permission for the pipe to be laid through any intervening land. At Waverley in 1215, when the spring from which the monks obtained their supply suddenly dried up, "not without great astonishment," Symon the monk searched and at last found a spring six hundred yards from the east end of the buildings. "After great difficulty, enquiry and invention, and not without much labour and sweating he brought it by underground channels to the offices of the abbey." It was usual first to make an accumulating cistern at the source and then convey the water through lead pipes (which were welded, not drawn) to a conduit and there re-distribute it to the various offices. At Beaulieu, hollowed

111 FOUNTAINS ABBEY, YORKSHIRE (*Cistercian*): the Warming Room

112 GLOUCESTER CATHEDRAL ABBEY (*Benedictine*): the Cloister Carrels for Study

113 HAUGHMOND ABBEY, SHROPSHIRE (*Augustinian*):
the Kitchen Chimneys

114 TORRE ABBEY, DEVON (*Premonstratensian*): the Undercroft

elm trunks were used for the main supply to the conduit-house; the latter still exists, circular in plan, twelve feet in diameter, with a plain domed roof. Gloucester had two supplies, one for drinking and washing, the other for flushing the drains, with an arrangement for that purpose. Westminster obtained its supply from the Serpentine, and other excellent supplies were at Durham (100), Mount-Grace, Rievaulx, Winchester and Worcester.

Another plan, dated 1431, exists for the supply to the Charterhouse in London. This was of an elaborate nature and travelled underground for over a mile, having a series of traps, air-boxes, suspirals and receptacles. Permission had to be obtained for carriage through other people's property, or gifts of land secured. The various agreements included "free laying of tubes of lead, leave to dig for laying and to cover them with clay, stones or wood, with free access or egress for their workmen and servants. They were to have free access to examine and repair when necessary, but were to pay for any damage to crops and grass caused thereby." William Symmes and Anne Tatersale gave 300 marks towards the cost; also 220 marks for the purchase of rents for the repair and maintenance of the aforesaid conduit. Reading had two sources of supply, one for domestic purposes, the other for turning the mill and flushing the sewer. The water was brought from Whitley by two-inch leaden pipes which passed under the Kennet; it was cold and clear and had a reputation for being good for sore and weak eyes.

A stream for clearing the drainage was an essential when choosing a site for a monastery. It was split up so as to run under the rere-dorter, infirmary and kitchens. Many of the underground passages which the ciceroni tell their flocks were secret passages to a neighbouring nunnery or castle are really the remains of great drains. Split streams and drainage systems can be studied in the ruined abbeys of Furness, Whalley and elsewhere. If a stream ran through a city before entering the precincts it was inevitably foul and had to be cleaned out at heavy expense. At Winchester an iron grating was fixed in the south exit lest the horrors should pass out from the priory precincts. On account of this stream and the quarrels it provoked, the transepts at Winchester were not converted into the later style as was the nave.

It was due to the fostering care of the monasteries and the bishops, and the commissions of royalty, that craftsmen were able to develop and continue their work. The size of this book precludes an investigation of their activities; Lethaby has done justice to some of them in his interesting volume on *Westminster Abbey and the Kings' Craftsmen*. Apart from the finer arts there was constant employment for glaziers, plumbers, smiths and bell-founders. The chronicle of Croxden tells the story of the founding of their bell in 1313. "The great bell was broken on the vigil of Easter, and master Henry of Lichfield came to cast another, and laboured at it with his men from the octave of Trinity until the feast of the Nativity of the Blessed Virgin and then failed in casting it, losing all his labour and costs. But having made ready afresh a great part of the brass and tin and beginning the whole business again, at length he finished the bell as it is now heard, about the feast of All Saints." During the fourteenth century a certain monk of Combermere, known as Thomas the plummer, was working for no less than 166 days in a single year for the king upon the lead roofs of Chester and Beeston Castles; he received eightpence a day for himself and his assistant. As Combermere was a Cistercian monastery, no doubt Thomas was a lay-brother lent out by the abbot at the request of the authorities, his wages going to the funds of the house.

115 Reredorter of the Conversi

116 Dorter of the Conversi
FOUNTAINS ABBEY, YORKSHIRE (*Cistercian*)

117 FOUNTAINS ABBEY, YORKSHIRE (*Cistercian*): Undercroft of Conversi, originally divided up

CHAPTER SEVEN

SOCIAL REACTIONS

IN the first flush of their enthusiasm the monasteries more than justified their existence. They were the fortresses amidst a world of savagery, where learning was preserved, worship continued and the arts encouraged. They taught the Western world the uses of agriculture in supplying the needs of men, instead of having to rely upon the chase. By their example they gradually educated the people in law and order, and the advantages of a continuous system in place of the haphazard methods then prevalent. The Benedictines lived where folk congregated; or if not, towns soon sprang up under the shadow of their walls. The Cistercians dwelt in the country, cultivating the waste places and bringing them into profitable use. Both produced noble architecture, orderly and well built, and proved by well-conducted houses the value of permanence in a world more or less nomadic in its habits.

The monasteries for many centuries were in advance of their time in the planning, furnishing and conduct of their houses. They were the only places where the inhabitants lived according to a rule, each individual having specific duties assigned to him; in which accounts were kept and a community of men dwelt together in amity, and in which every little difference did not end in strife and bloodshed. The monastery was a house of well-ordered quietness, and it is not surprising that men fled to these oases in a desert of tumult; for a military profession was the only one open to a noble or a freeman, and learning apart from religion was almost unknown.

The monasteries also espoused the honour of labour, then considered only fit for slaves or serfs. They taught it by example, tilling the fields and gardens, doing humble work of all kinds, worshipping God whilst labouring in the fields as well as in the church. These early ideals were not however of long continuance, for as they became wealthy and powerful, their rigid code of behaviour fell into abeyance. The popularity gained by demonstrating the possibility of living for God in a world of iniquity proved their undoing. Lands and money were lavished upon them, and they became tainted with the world and its ways. Again and again new Orders arose, each harking back to first principles; but as each grew in wealth the original ideal faded as a dream. To the last however they retained many good points; they still stood for communism, though of an aristocratic type; but with their failure to guide their usefulness ceased. By then, however, the world had learnt much of what they had to teach and had caught up with them. The fault of the Orders until the coming of the friars was that they looked inward instead of outward, being more interested in saving their whole souls than in leavening the masses. As they ignored the needs of the world, so in their day of trial the world ignored them. If the Orders had adhered to their principles, there would have been no suppression; but their wealth filled the unprincipled kings and nobles with cupidity, and in the end proved their ruin.

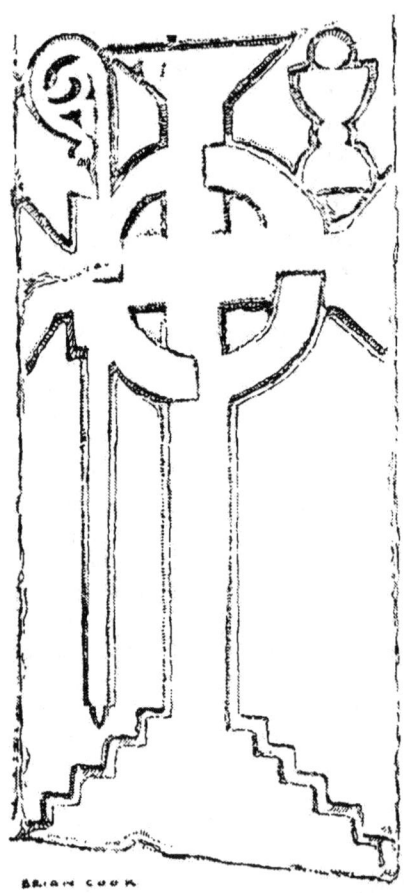

BLANCHLAND, CO. DURHAM: INCISED SEPULCHRAL SLAB WITH PASTORAL STAFF AND CHALICE

LITERATURE AND THE ARTS.—The monastic libraries contained practically all the wealth of medieval literature, both in variety of content and in beauty of script and illumination. Many monks devoted a lifetime to the production of a single volume such as the Winchester Bible, which remained unfinished at the writer's death. The abbey of St. Alban was famous not only for the production of books, but for its services to the writers, of whom Wendover and Matthew Paris may be singled out. Their chronicles still remain

118　WATTON ABBEY, YORKSHIRE (*Gilbertian*): the Abbot's Lodging

119　CASTLE ACRE, NORFOLK (*Cluniac*): the Prior's Lodging

120 MUCH WENLOCK, SHROPSHIRE (*Cluniac*) : the Prior's Lodging

121 ELY CATHEDRAL ABBEY (*Benedictine*): Prior's Lodging and Crauden's Chapel

122 CHESTER ABBEY (*Benedictine*): a Grange belonging to the Abbey at Saighton

the foundations upon which writers on medieval times build their knowledge. The size of monastic libraries can be gauged by the catalogue of the Canterbury manuscripts, made between 1285 and 1331 which enumerates 1850. Durham possessed 921 volumes, and several catalogues from other convents show how large was their scope. All these libraries remained until the suppression, when they were either wilfully destroyed or dispersed. The treasures still extant would have been even less had not some of the religious at the time bought volumes for their own use, which have since found their way into national and college libraries.

The monasteries were filled with the work of contemporary craftsmen who, but for their patronage, would never have had the chance to develop their art. The work commissioned included that of the glass-workers, craftsmen and carvers in wood, stone and ivory, smiths, painters and artists, gold and silver workers, tapestry weavers and embroiderers. Hence the establishment of gilds of craftsmen owing their origin and livelihood to the orders given by the religious. Employment was found for large numbers of masons, tilers, lead-workers and carpenters, many of whose names have been collected by Lethaby in his books on Westminster Abbey.

HOSPITALITY AND ALMSGIVING.—In the matter of hospitality the monasteries were the hotels and inns of the Middle Ages; they seem never to have been without guests, welcome and unwelcome. The ordered existence combined with the material comforts provided was an education as well as a protest against the vices and improvidence of the age. It must have had a leavening influence on the royalty and nobles coming within their sphere, whose irresponsible methods of living were a constant menace to the stability of the country. Naturally the monastic hospitality was abused, for it must have been a luxury to stay in the noble guest-houses, well furnished and clean, with food properly cooked and served with due regard to etiquette and the observances of decency, in place of the rough roistering which took place in the castles, where the contents of half-emptied dishes were thrown amongst the rushes on the floor for the dogs. The upper classes were often entertained at the abbot's table, and the feasts recorded in the chronicles are incredible in the quantities of food consumed. The wealthier travellers were housed in the guest-houses, and the poor, palmers, pilgrims and the like in the almonries, and fed literally from the crumbs which fell from the rich men's tables.

The record of their almsgiving is not impressive. The monks supported certain numbers of old bedesmen and women in almshouses and in the almonries, and at obits and anniversaries distributed bread, and occasionally money, while well-worn clothes were given to the poor. They were supposed to visit the sick in the neighbourhood of the monasteries and give them assistance, but this seems to have been more the exception than the rule; more often they took colour from the surrounding world in their outlook towards the downtrodden, and their sympathy towards the stricken was finer in theory than in practice. The medieval world was a sorry place for people without influence and without means; the monks like laymen followed the precept that a man should be content with the place God had provided for him, and not allow his mind to dwell on better things. This attitude towards the poorer folk is to be found in the constant injunctions made in the Observances, to watch carefully that the servants do not steal, idle or misbehave, and to be careful to choose men who were not given to lying and drunkenness; for what is only amusing in the noble becomes a crime when practised by his servants. The manners of the age were primitive; even an ecclesiastic could push another off his seat when he considered his precedence was at stake, or sit on the other's knees, an incident which took place at a meeting when both archbishops were present. It was a hard bullying age, and it is to the credit of the religious that they were generally more enlightened than the laymen, and practised at least some of the Christian virtues.

Neither did the monasteries take a strong lead in educational matters. They had houses in the university towns and sent their more intellectual novices to study either there or in Paris, but the number was never large, and many houses sent none. They certainly taught the novices, and had a school for their singing boys, but the outside world did not share in these benefits to any great extent. Sometimes poor boys were taught in the almonry; there are records of free schools attached to the monasteries, and in certain towns grammar schools were founded by the abbots. These increased in number towards the close of the Middle Ages. When the suppression came, many of them were refounded by the despoilers and re-christened with their own names, but often

123 MUCHELNEY ABBEY, SOMERSET
(*Benedictine*): the Abbot's Lodging

124 GLASTONBURY ABBEY, SOMERSET
(*Benedictine*): the Commandery, where the Abbot tried his tenants, etc.

125 HAUGHMOND ABBEY, SHROPSHIRE (*Augustinian*):
Remains of the Infirmary

126 BRADFORD ABBAS, WILTSHIRE. Barn belonging to
the Abbey of Shaftesbury

with curtailed endowments. We do not possess sufficient records to know how far the monks went in this matter, but the item quoted from the Westminster *compotus* rolls relating to little Nigel tends to show that in certain circumstances the monastic officials were sympathetic towards children.

LANDLORDS AND AGRICULTURISTS.—The monasteries from the first were landowners, for the founders endowed them with lands, which were increased from time to time by gifts made for the saving of the souls of the donors. These lands were brought into cultivation by the monks and were divided into three classes: waste, arable and pasture, the tenants of each manor having shares in each class. The waste land was by far the largest and was common to all for the pasturing of cattle, cutting of turves, gathering of wood and mowing of hay. Such commons remaining to us are the remnants of the original waste land of early times. In time the abbeys brought more land into cultivation by clearing, ploughing and marling, making for the purpose clay-pits, which afterwards became the ponds still to be seen in the fields. This progress was discouraged by the realm and the lords by heavy fines imposed on any person who cultivated a new piece of land, especially if it interfered with hunting or encroached upon forests; the tenants also objected to forfeit their rights in the common lands. The arable land was held jointly by the abbot and his tenants. It was cultivated in long strips about 220 yards in length by $5\frac{1}{2}$ in width, each strip a quarter of an acre in extent, separated from each other by ridges of turf thrown up by ploughing. The whole was ploughed by the common ploughs, the tenants providing the oxen. During the growing of the crops the arable land was fenced in from cattle, the headlands becoming recognised lanes with rights of way, the double right-hand turnings in some of our old lanes being thus accounted for. When the crops were gathered, fences were thrown down and the cattle allowed to wander over the land until the next sowing, forming a primitive method of manuring. Under this system little individuality could be exercised, and every tenant was bound to work for the common good. The meadowland was cultivated in strips and fenced until the hay-crop was gathered, after which it became common pasture.

There were two differing types of tenants belonging to a manor: money tenants and service tenants. The former, called the *censarii*, paid a money rent and were freed from the work required from the second class, but they had to find oxen for ploughing and extra labour for harvest. The service tenants were called villeins and usually held two bovates of land, eight bovates being enough for one plough. Their service was to work two days a week, find carts for carting, to plough twice a year and reap thrice in August, to fetch salt and fish and to pay for the use of the abbot's pasture land; and there were many restrictions and fines. Villeins could be sold with an estate, but could not be sold as chattels; they had also to pay a fine for obtaining the abbot's consent to a daughter's marriage. Comparing the position of the villeins on the manors of the lords, the convents, and the king, Coulton thinks that the monastic villeins were better off than under the lords but not so well off as under the king. The religious were more humane in their treatment, but this was counterbalanced by their innate conservativeness; the manner of treatment depended also upon the individual character of the abbot. At Titchfield, at harvest-time those who worked a whole day received at 3 p.m. bread with either beer or cider, broth and two sorts of meat or fish, as well as a drink after dinner; for supper a wheaten loaf of forty ounces and either two herrings, four pilchards or one mackerel. The liberality of the food supplied by Battle to service tenants exceeded the value of the labour rendered. No food was given on secular manors except on special occasions. The monastic tenant had on the whole more liberty and leniency shown him and was more prosperous than the tenant on the secular manor.

Other tenants were the *bovarii* and the *cotsetti*. The former looked after the abbot's ploughs and oxen, and generally held two bovates of land; the latter were the cottagers and labourers who worked one day a week for the abbot. Finally came the actual slaves or *servii* who were liable for service and held no connection with the land; they were bought and sold as mere chattels; but it is considered by some authorities that this class was extinct towards the close of the thirteenth century. All these grades of tenants were in a state of bondage or serfdom, though in some degree removed from actual slavery. It is curious that in the eyes of the law they all had very few liberties, but in actual practice they enjoyed by custom substantial rights. But the following instances show the insecurity of the rural workers' legal position and the tendency of the monasteries to push to the uttermost what they considered their legal rights even in regard to the lives of their workers and their children. At Whalley in

127 CANTERBURY CATHEDRAL ABBEY (*Benedictine*):
Entrance to Almonry

128 CANTERBURY CATHEDRAL ABBEY (*Benedictine*):
Brew and Bakehouse of the Prior

129 EVESHAM ABBEY, WORCESTERSHIRE (*Benedictine*):
the Almonry

1289 a serf was sold for 100 shillings with all his brood. William Dives gave the monks of Eynsham, "Richard Rowland, who was my born serf with all his brood." At Winchester in the fifteenth century the convent went to considerable expense to prove that John Boys with all his progeny was their property. A manorial tenant could not leave the estate upon which he was born, and if he did he was fined as at Winchester, in 1539, where two named Prior were fined for settling down outside the manor. Serfdom was one of the iniquities of the feudal system, but in time the serfs became fewer in number, gradually buying their freedom. Their position is shown in a plea by the Abbot of Kirkstall against Thomas de Eltoft and two others, who forcibly rescued Robert Bateman, a native of the abbot, who for a certain act of rebellion had put him in the stocks in order to have him whipped.

The abbot had a steward or bailiff to manage his various manors and to watch the under-bailiffs. He presided at the manor courts when the abbot did not attend in person. The abbot kept his own gallows and stocks and maintained order through his own officials. As Hibbert puts it so well, "The whole organisation, social, agricultural, economic, centred round the monastic owners, and was framed primarily to fulfil their requirements. When the land had to be ploughed the abbot's demesne was ploughed by the tenants, drawn by their oxen, and tended by their labourers. It was harrowed and hoed by tenant service, though sown by the abbot's servants with the abbey corn. The arable part of the folkland was similarly ploughed by the common ploughs, but sown at the expense of the tenants. The reaping was largely done by the services of the tenants who also did the carting." If the services were not performed, the land reverted back to the abbot. The tenants lived in small villages and appointed their ablest man to look after their interests. He was named the foreman or reeve and was often in opposition to the bailiff. The villagers also combined together in employing a herdsman, shepherd and swine-herd.

The abbot's woods brought in revenues, especially in the autumn when the mast or beech-nuts and acorns fell. All villagers kept pigs, which generally had to find their own living; but in the autumn, by payment either in money or in kind, the villagers were allowed the privilege of turning their swine into the woods. In 1279 the pannage of the woods was handed to the Abbot of Vale Royal, who received sixty-two and sixpence and eighty pigs valued at eight pounds. In 1325 the abbot sold the season's acorns of Bradford Wood to Richard of Buckelegh, who turned forty swine into the wood. A neighbouring squire broke down the fences, seized Richard's swine and put fifty of his own in their place. The abbot's servants seized these pigs and the squire then entered into litigation with the abbot, but failed. The abbot's woods were useful for hunting, providing a pastime for himself and his friends. In 1258 there was a dispute between Hugh, prior of Kirkham, and William de Rhos, as to the right of the prior, who was hunting in the said wood with his dogs, "to wit limers, brachets and hare hounds, and taking all manner of beasts, to wit stags, harts, hinds, foxes and hares. The prior says his predecessors have hunted time beyond memory until five years ago."

In reading of what took place during the attempts made by the people to free themselves from the heavy yoke imposed upon them by the feudal system, it must be remembered that the monasteries were only a part of that system. Unfortunately they tried no fresh schemes to help humanity, remaining conservative to the last in maintaining their legal rights. Medieval society was disorderly, and the example set by the better classes did not help. Some districts were worse than others, Cheshire in particular being the home of a fierce, quarrelsome, turbulent and restive race, difficult to control but excellent in warfare.

The Peasants' Rising and the general unrest in the fourteenth century led to acts of brutality on both sides in which the abbeys shared. The trouble began as early as 1229 at Dunstable, where there was a rebellion over tallage, the rebels declaring when excommunicated, that they would go to hell sooner than be beaten. In 1236 the villeins of Abbots Bromley brought an action against their abbot, claiming the rights as free tenants; but the verdict went against them. In 1280 Burton did the same but were also beaten. In 1309 the Abbot of Combermere was assaulted at Nantwich, one of his monks slain, his grange burnt, and his goods stolen. During the enquiry the people took on such a threatening attitude that the abbot dared not return to his abbey. In 1330 at Vale Royal one of the abbot's servants was murdered, and the men who assaulted him cut off his head and played football with it. In 1381 at Bury the serfs and the bondsmen condemned the prior during a rebellion and cut off his head. Bishop Norbury

130 BURY ST. EDMUNDS ABBEY, SUFFOLK (*Benedictine*):
Gateway

131 BURY ST. EDMUNDS ABBEY, SUFFOLK: Norman Gateway

denounced the men who had injured the Prior of Sandwell's property and that of his tenants, and had assaulted a friar at Lichfield. We have already seen how the villeins of Whaplode treated the steward of Crowland in the fifteenth century. There was a general spirit of lawlessness abroad.

A striking instance in this struggle for freedom was made by the villeins of Darnhall, a manor of Vale Royal. As early as the founder's days they appealed to the king against the oppression of the abbot but without success; they made further complaint in 1307 with the same result. In 1329 they broke into open insurrection, and were tried by the abbot's court, not as plaintiffs, but as prisoners judged by the defendant. They were put in shackles and their property confiscated. In 1336 a renewal of their appeal to the king and parliament met with the same fate; however, meeting the abbot who barely escaped with his life, on his return through Rutland, they killed his groom. They were then hauled before the king at Stamford, and compelled to make abject submission. The scales of justice, as they had always been, were heavily weighted against them, and the struggle they began took centuries to bring to fruition.

THE STATUTE OF MORTMAIN.—The statute of mortmain introduced by Edward I was an attempt to stop any further gifts of land to religious foundations, but if such gifts were made, a licence was required, an enquiry held and fines paid. In its primary object it may be said to have failed, for lands and money continued to be given as before, but in other ways it was successful, for it placed the power to control the gifts in the hands of the Crown. Although often attempted this law was found impossible to evade, and there was the added penalty, that all estates given without a licence were forfeit to the Crown.

Gifts were not often made to monastic houses unconditionally, they were generally given to secure masses being said for the souls of the donors and their ancestors, and if given without a licence the forfeiture which ensued annulled the object of the gift, thereby imperilling the souls of the benefactors. This law made it more difficult to present land or money. Upon application for a licence the sheriff had to call together a jury to examine all the facts, assess the value of the gift, and estimate how far the Crown was being deprived of taxes and emoluments, and in the event of a licence being granted, the size of the fine had to be fixed. These fines do not appear to have borne any relation to the value of the land, and we do not know by what methods they were levied. In many instances, however, people who had benefited the State were let off lightly, especially if the king was interested in the house. Monasteries also acquired land by purchase and seem to have had no difficulty in raising money for this purpose when lands adjacent to their estates came into the market. They also exchanged lands when mutually beneficial, and made pensions and small grants to bishops and others in compensation for appropriated churches. In all these cases a licence had to be obtained.

The Crown in this way acquired power over the activities of religious houses. In view of the pious nature of donations, prohibition of benefactions would have raised a storm from the clergy and laity alike; but the Crown obtained power to ensure that the donor's stipulations were carried out. If it was proved that these conditions had been neglected, the gift could be made void. If the gift was entered upon before the licence was granted and the fine paid, a pardon had to be sought, and when granted, involved further expense. The giving of a chantry for the repose of the souls of the donors was often of a selfish nature. In the appropriation of a church for such a purpose, neither rector nor parish were consulted, but had to acquiesce with the best grace they could.

MONASTERIES IN THE TOWNS.—The association of a monastery with a town in which it was placed grew difficult as the town developed, and led either to riotous behaviour or a sullen resistance to the rights of the abbot. At first the villages were glad of their protection, the domination of an abbey being a help; but as trade developed the burgesses became restive and attempted to free themselves from the abbot's restrictions, with his rights of toll and fairs, fees and elections. The chronicles of Bury contain many references to disputes between the town and the convent in 1264, 1292, 1305, terminating in 1327 in riots and rebellion, when the abbey was plundered, most of the buildings burnt, and the abbot seized and deported to France.

Reading remained under the rule of the abbot for 250 years. During the whole time the abbot maintained all his rights, the town struggling unsuccessfully to throw them off, resulting in constant friction and disputes. The inhabitants were bound hand and foot, for he was the owner of the streams, fisheries, mills and soil. He held the markets, controlled trade and supervised the manufacture of cloth; he appointed the mayor and lesser officials, exercising his veto for admission to the gild. The entire administration of justice was in his hands, fines being imposed for any and every breach of his laws, and he reserved to himself the symbols of office. The constant appeals to the king were unavailing, for the king and the abbot worked together for a common end. All abbots were not however like those of Bury and Reading; at Burton they seem to have been fairly popular throughout the whole period. They built and paved the streets, provided a market hall and a conduit, and later founded a grammar school. As towns developed resentment was felt against the right of the abbots to hold fairs. There were complaints from the burgesses of Stafford, Lichfield and Tutbury concerning the fairs at Burton and Abbots Bromley. In 1281 the friars of Stafford claimed the king's protection from the common hucksters and the following year stated that they were prevented from buying their victuals, or that when they did so, these were snatched out of their hands. The abbey of Chester to some extent escaped the bitter hostility shown elsewhere. Defeated in their early attempts to enlarge their trading rights they made concessions and tried to conciliate the burgesses. They also provided mystery plays for the gratification of the town and in other ways maintained goodwill.

The monasteries helped the towns in other ways. Where their estates came up against the city walls, it was their duty to keep them in repair and provide defenders as well as defences, as at Chester and Winchester. The Prior of Dover in 1476 was called upon to keep the town's cannon "ready with powder and stones and other stuff as they used to do in times past." The maintenance of bridges and roads were religious duties, the abbots doing their share, especially when they connected up their estates. At Ely, which was surrounded by fen and swamp, they built several bridges and constructed roads to enable pilgrims to reach the monastery, every bridge having its toll-keeper, the revenues going to the sacrist. In the fourteenth century the Abbot of Chester made an agreement with the neighbouring lords as to the repair of several bridges in the district. In 1283 Crowland and Spalding constructed many bridges. In the thirteenth century the Abbot of Whitby built a permanent bridge over the Esk. On the other hand the Abbot of Fountains in 1313 refused to repair the bridge at Bradeley, and in 1368 the Prior of Nostell was ordered to repair two bridges at Birstall and Batley, being the rector of both places, but complained that none of his predecessors had been bound to do so.

MONASTIC RELATIONS.—The relations between monastic houses were not always smooth. The tenacity shown in adhering to rights against outside interference was carried into their relations with each other, and many cases of litigation occurred. The Cistercian abbey of Sawley appealed against one of their own Order founding a house as near as Whalley; but there does not seem to have been any trouble between Rievaulx and Byland, who were in even closer proximity. Matters only became serious when there was a struggle between a daughter- and mother-house to gain independence, sometimes owing to wrongly worded charters. Monk Bretton was founded under the Cluniac Pontefract, the head of Cluny giving Bretton the right to elect its own prior, should the Prior of Pontefract be present. To this Pontefract would not agree and the most unseemly quarrels with armed interference took place, especially when Pontefract took possession of Bretton and imprisoned the monks. Papal bulls and verdicts of commissions had no effect on this state of affairs, which after temporary lulls broke out with added bitterness, Pontefract electing priors from their own house, Bretton repudiating them. Finally Bretton seceded from the Cluniacs and joined the Benedictines with the help of the Archbishop of York, but for many years the atmosphere created continued to affect the house; priors being deposed and the monks remaining contumacious.

Dover Priory was refounded by the king as an independent house with power to elect its own prior, but was placed under the protection of the Archbishop of Canterbury. During a vacancy the monks of Canterbury claimed the right to govern the priory and to elect its head, which right was stoutly disputed by Dover, who appealed to the King, the Pope and others. However, Canterbury continued to elect priors from their own house and to interfere with Dover affairs. It was not as fortunate as Bretton and was finally subjected to Canterbury.

RELATIONS WITH NOBLES AND LORDS.—Monastic relations with the lords surrounding their demesnes can be judged in two ways, by gifts made to them and the litigation which took place between them. Both were numerous, but the latter makes the more interesting reading. Owing to the loose way

132 THORNTON ABBEY, LINCOLNSHIRE (*Augustinian*):
the Gateway of Brick and Stone

133 ST. OSYTH'S ABBEY, ESSEX (*Augustinian*): the Gateway of Flint and Stone

134 BATTLE ABBEY, SUSSEX (*Benedictine*): the Gateway

135 WORKSOP PRIORY, NOTTINGHAMSHIRE (*Augustinian*): the Gateway

in which lands were defined there was constant friction and charges of trespass; rights of way were disputed, and the question of responsibility for the repair of roads and bridges led to quarrels. The lords of the manors, though aristocratic, were generally ill-mannered, often taking the law into their own hands. With a hot-tempered master, the armed retainers like schoolboys ready for a fight, were generally in trouble.

In 1277 the Abbot of St. Agatha's sued Henry de Stanley and others for throwing down the abbot's mill at Chardehale, and doing other enormities to the damage of a hundred shillings. In 1320 a plea was lodged on behalf of John Lewis, cellarer of Vale Royal, who on his return after transacting business in Chester, was set upon at Tarvin by seven men from Northwich, and barely escaped with his life. In 1334 the Prior of Tutbury was captured on his way home from visiting the bishop, and the men were solemnly cursed from the altar. At Croxden in 1319 the new lord of Alverton demanded from the monks a daily distribution of alms, the keeping of his horses and hounds to any number he pleased, the maintaining every Friday of seven of his bailiffs with a room for their use. On refusal he captured a hundred and sixty of the convent's sheep, twenty oxen and thirty-two horses, so that the monks were unable to plough or sow. In 1340 Peter, abbot of Vale Royal, and a fellow monk were murdered, and in 1342 the Abbot of Byland sued fourteen men, "who by force of arms did break the banks of the river Derwent at Rillington, by which the water issued from the breaches and so flooded the abbot's pasture that there was a loss of ten pounds." In 1375 a group of relations of the Buckeley family of Cheadle, Cheshire, assaulted a mason who, they thought, was employed at Vale Royal, and further laid in wait nearby the abbey, ill-treating the monks, so that no one dare leave the convent, and the inmates were in danger of starvation.

In 1426 Hugh Venables of Kinderton Hall, having fallen foul of Vale Royal about fishing rights, took revenge by plundering one of the granges and driving off cattle worth 100 marks: "on Shrove Thursday, not dreading God, he maimed the abbot's bailiff and left him for dead. In Easter week he broke into the mill and hacked the machinery to pieces and with his retainers laid in wait day and night to maim the monks and their servants, and to slay the abbot. They were so frightened that they dare not minister to the said abbey during this time of dread." The king wrote a series of letters to Venables without effect, finally ordering the justices of Chester to punish Hugh and keep him in prison, "for the great riots, extorcions and oppressions and the horrible and cruel murders he has done to the officers, tenants and servants of the said monastery."

THE SUPPRESSION.—The suppression of the monasteries was not without precedent. It had been done more than once. The whole order of Knights Templars was suppressed by the Pope in 1309. Again, towards the end of the fourteenth century alien priories were suppressed in England during the king's wars abroad, although many of them survived by affiliating themselves to English Orders. In the early years of the sixteenth century Cardinal Wolsey, to further his scheme for the founding of Cardinal College at Oxford, suppressed a number of the lesser houses. Had these principles guided the general suppression and had the greater monasteries been utilised for the founding of colleges and cathedrals, England would have been in the forefront of learning and the arts in Europe. But such schemes were far from the minds of the king and his satellites, who were actuated solely by vindictiveness and cupidity; the first because the king had been thwarted in his wishes by the Church, and the second with the object of replenishing his impoverished exchequer.

Whatever excuses may be brought forward for the suppression of the monasteries, the callous manner in which it was performed cannot be forgiven. The religious were expelled from their houses, those who were renegades were given small allowances, while those who refused to desert their principles were hanged, drawn and quartered. The priceless treasures of learning and art of five hundred years were wantonly destroyed or dispersed; the illuminated manuscripts were sold to grocers and others for wrapping butter; their buildings, representing some of the finest architectural efforts of the Middle Ages, were thrown down. What could be sold was sold, and the patrimony of the monks divided between the jackals who dogged the heels of a splendthrift monarch. The men who were really advantaged were the commissioners and agents of the king, who first received gifts from the abbeys for promises of continued existence, and later bribes from the jackals waiting to divide the spoils.

Evil bred evil, and having despoiled the monasteries, the heads of the State turned towards other possible sources of

136 WALTHAM ABBEY, ESSEX (*Augustinian*): Bridge and Gateway

137 BURY ST. EDMUNDS ABBEY, SUFFOLK (*Benedictine*): the Abbot's Bridge

138 ROCHE ABBEY, YORKSHIRE (*Cistercian*). Air View from the South

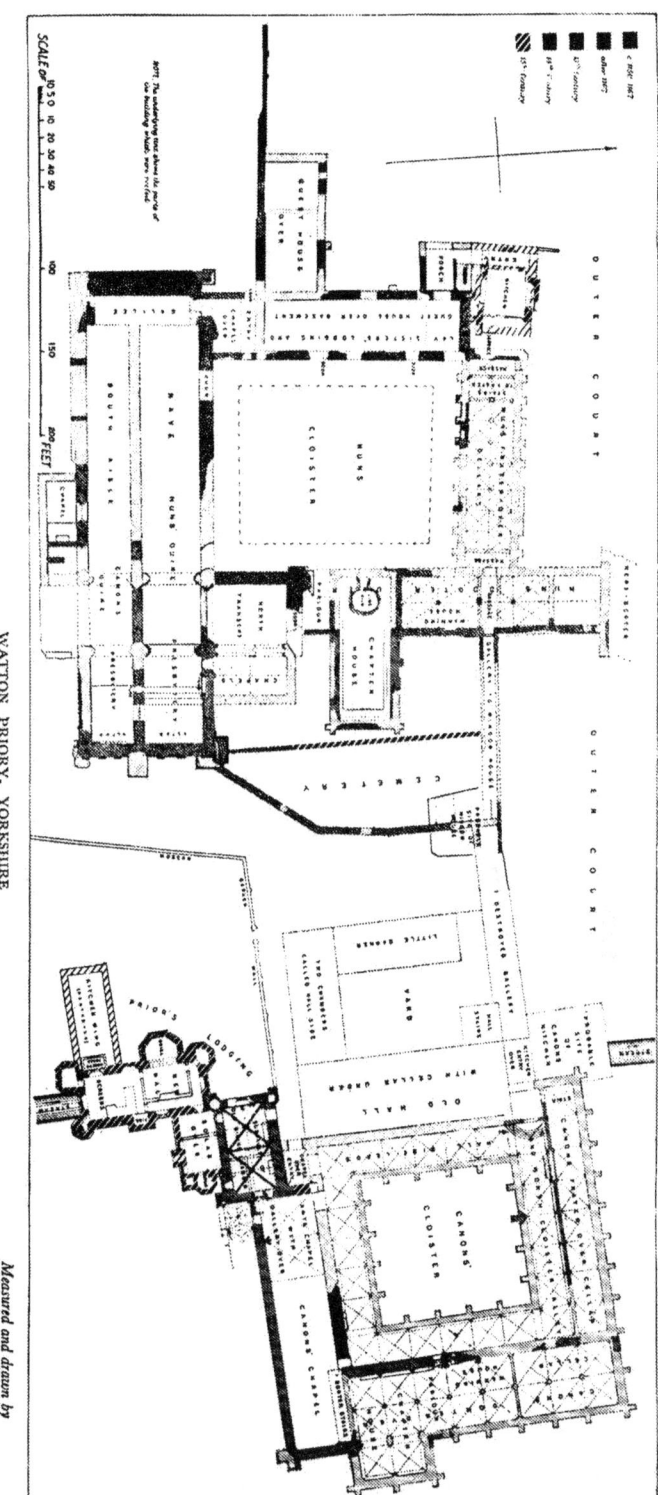

WATTON PRIORY, YORKSHIRE
(GILBERTINE)

Measured and drawn by
Sir W. H. St. John Hope
and Harold Brakspear

revenue. The suppression of the gilds and chantries followed, with the appropriation of their goods, but the lost tythes of the churches were not restored to them. The valuables belonging to the cathedrals and parish churches were next confiscated. During these times religion suffered a severe shock which was reflected in the lax morals of the age. The type of priest appointed to the cure of souls was such that Bishop Hooper in his visitation to his diocese of Gloucester found 168 priests who could not say the Ten Commandments, and thirty who did not know the author of the Lord's Prayer. The small isolated chapels fell into decay; for there were no religious orders to find priests for them. Although appropriated parish churches under monastic rule had not been in an enviable position, it was worse under the lay-patrons who followed them, often placing their own servants in the cures and collecting the emoluments into their own pockets. The Church entered upon a hundred years of disquiet and dissension, dragged first in one direction, then pushed in another, until it remained a wonder that religion survived.

EPILOGUE

IN such a small book it is only possible to give the main outlines of the subject, illustrated by extracts and quotations. There is a mass of information left over for those who are interested and who desire further information. Many scholars have devoted both time and patience to elucidating medieval documents and rolls, which are generally stored more or less in inaccessible places, translating portions of them for the benefit of students. Others have excavated the sites of monastic buildings and with infinite care have collected the information produced, making large-scale plans of the various ruins. Between them they have laid the foundations for a fairly complete study of monachism in England. These essays are for the most part scattered in the volumes of Transactions issued by various Archaeological Societies, or if in book form have been issued to subscribers in small numbers.

I append a list of the publications without which it would not have been possible to write this book, and I offer to the writers my gratitude and thanks. It seemed a hopeless task to write and ask each scholar for his permission to quote from his work; moreover, many of them are no longer with us, but by the following list and by this acknowledgment I hope to make a well-deserved recognition. I feel sure that their aim was the dissemination of knowledge, and it has been my endeavour to assist in the undertaking.

Rev. J. A. Giles, D.C.L.	*The Chronicles of Matthew Paris*	1889
Sir E. Clarke, M.A., F.S.A.	*The Chronicles of Jocelin of Brakelond*	1903
G. W. Kitchin, D.D., F.S.A.	*The Compotus Rolls of Winchester*	1892
F. R. Chapman, M.A.	*The Sacrist Rolls of Ely*	1907
J. Brownbill, M.A.	*The Leger Book of Vale Royal*	1914
Rev. Canon Fowler	*The Rites of Durham*	1902
J. W. Clarke, M.A., F.S.A.	*The Observances of Barnwell*	1897
J. W. Wilson, D.D.	*The Worcester Liber Albus*	1919–20
F. M. Powicke, M.A., LIT.D.	*Ailred of Rievaulx*	1922
Abbot Gasquet, D.D.	*Henry the Third and the Church*	1905
K. L. Wood-Legh	*Studies in Church Life under Edward III*	1934
R. H. Snape, M.A.	*English Monastic Finance*	1926
D. Knoop, M.A., G. P. Jones, M.A.	*The Mediaeval Mason*	1933
G. Unwin, M.A.	*Finance and Trade under Edward III*	1918
H. J. Hewitt, M.A., PH.D.	*Mediaeval Cheshire*	1929
Rose Graham, F.S.A.	*St. Gilbert and the Gilbertines*	1901
Rev. D. J. Stewart, M.A., F.S.A.	*Ely Cathedral*	1868
Professor R. Willis, M.A., F.S.A.	*Canterbury Cathedral*	1845

W. Wallis, M.A.	*A History of the Church in Blackburnshire*	1932
F. A. Hibbert, M.A.	*Monasticism in Staffordshire*	1909
L. F. Salzman, M.A., F.S.A.	*English Industries in the Middle Ages*	1923
Sir St. John Hope, M.A.	*The Abbey of Furness*	1902
H. F. Westlake, M.A., F.S.A.	*Westminster Abbey*	1923
Professor W. R. Lethaby	*Westminster Abbey and the King's Craftsmen*	1906
Sir St. John Hope, M.A.	*The London Charterhouse*	1925
C. Lynam, F.S.A.	*Croxden Abbey*	1911
A. W. Clapham, F.S.A.	*Lesnes Abbey*	1915
C. R. Haines, M.A., F.S.A.	*Dover Priory*	1930
R. Stewart Brown, M.A.	*Birkenhead Priory*	1925
J. W. Walker, F.S.A.	*Priory of Monk Bretton*	1926
J. B. Hurry, M.A., M.D.	*Reading Abbey*	1901
Professor A. Hamilton Thompson	*English Monasteries*	1913
Abbot Gasquet, D.D.	*English Monastic Life*	1904
Dean Cranage, M.A., F.S.A.	*The Home of the Monk*	1926

SEPARATE PAPERS PRINTED IN JOURNALS

Rev. R. B. Rackham, "The Nave of Westminster," *British Academy*, 1909-10.
D. Knoop and G. P. Jones, "The First Three Years Building of Vale Royal," *Ars Quatuor Coronatorum*, Vol. 44.
Rev. H. V. Le Bas and Sir W. Hope, "Mount Grace Priory," *Yorkshire Archaeological Journal*, Vol. 18.
J. T. Micklethwaite, "Cistercian Order," *Yorkshire Archaeological Journal*, Vol. 15.
Sir W. Hope and H. Breakspear, "Beaulieu Abbey," *Archaeological Journal*, Vol. 63.
J. Bilson, "Architecture of the Cistercians," *Archaeological Journal*, Vol. 66.
Sir W. St. John Hope, "Fountains Abbey," *Yorkshire Archaeological. Journal*, Vol. 15.
Rye, "Rievaulx Canals and Building Stone," *Archaeological Journal*, Vol. 53.
W. A. Cater, "The London Austin Friars."

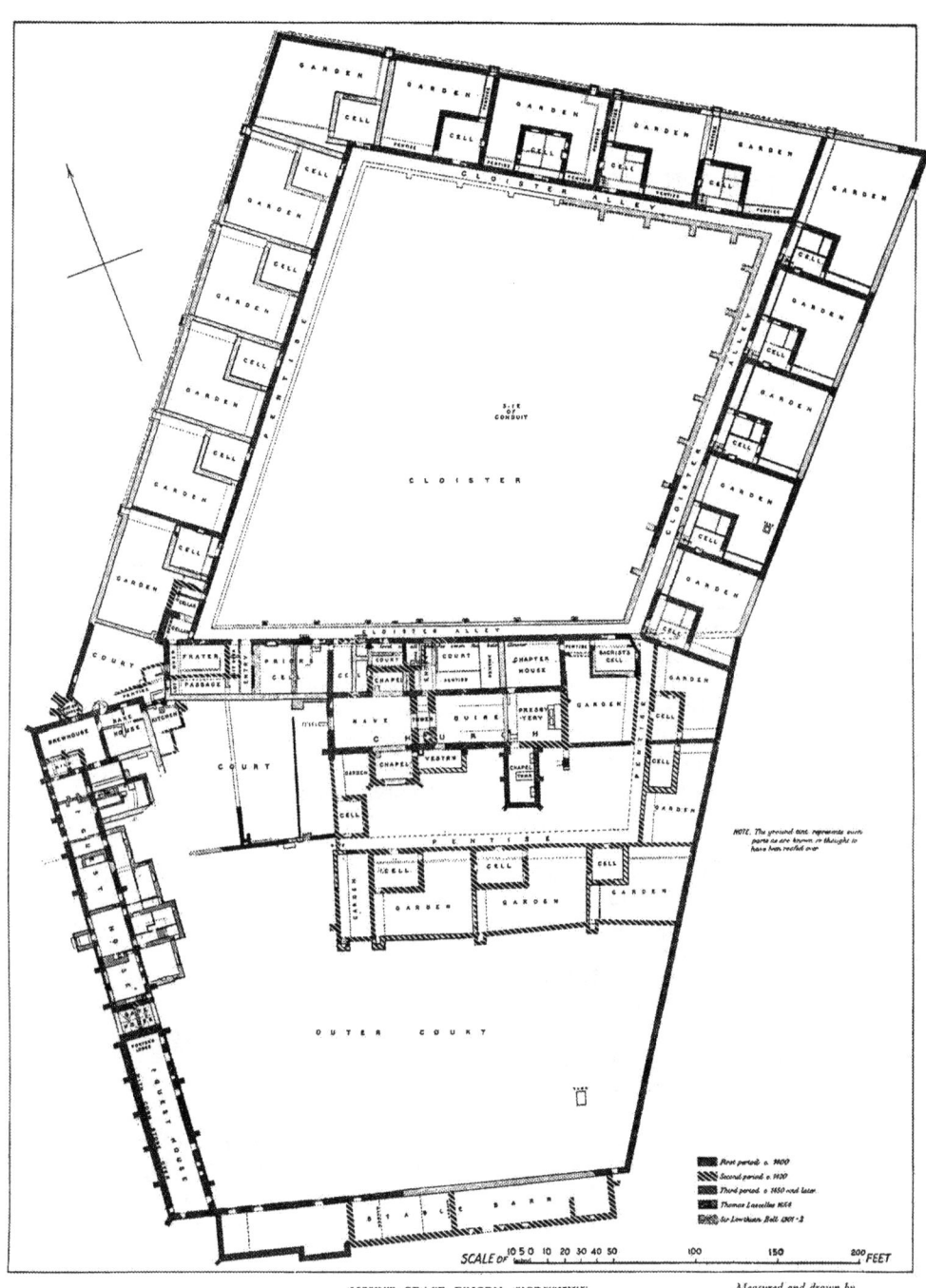

MOUNT GRACE PRIORY, YORKSHIRE
(CARTHUSIAN)

Measured and drawn by
Sir W. H. St. John Hope

INDEX

(The numerals in italic type denote the *figure numbers* of illustrations.)

Abbey Dore, 39; *45, 46*
Abbot—
  office of, 11, 12
  deposition of, 68
Abingdon, burial incident, 70
Administration, 65
Agriculture, 95
Ailred, Abbot of Rievaulx, 11
Almoner, office of, 25
Almsgiving, 94
Almshouses, 54
Appropriation of Churches, 70
Augustine, St., 2
  rule of, 6
Augustinian foundations—
  Bolton Priory, 6
  Bridlington Priory, *53*
  Brinkburn Priory, *63*
  Cartmel Priory, *62*
  Christchurch Priory, *61*
  Dunstable Priory, *76*
  Guisborough Priory, *22*
  Haughmond Abbey, *91, 113, 125*
  Hexham Priory, *43, 74, 98*
  Lacock Abbey, 7, 43; *90, 92*
  Lanercost Priory, *13*
  Llanthony Priory, *4, 64*
  Norton Priory, *38*
  St. Bartholomew's Priory, 6
  St. Botolph's Priory, *67*
  St. Germains Priory, *19*
  St. Osyth's Priory, *133*
  Thornton Abbey, *132*
  Walsingham Priory, *25*
  Waltham Abbey, *136*
  Woodspring Priory, *58*
  Worksop Priory, *14, 135*
Austin Friars, *53*

Bailiff—
  office of, 26
  in rioting, 27
Bath Abbey, *18*
Barnwell, observations of, 6, 13, 14, 17, 21, 24, 30, 94
Battle Abbey, *134*
Beaulieu Abbey, 36; *108*
Beer, 17, 22, 35
Bernard, St., Apologia of, 5
Benedict, St., 1
  rule of, 2
Benedictine foundations—
  Bath Abbey, *18*
  Battle Abbey, *134*
  Beaulieu Abbey, 36; *108*
  Birkenhead Priory, *93*
  Blythe Abbey, *56*
  Boxgrove Priory, *47*
  Bradford Abbas, *126*
  Buckfast Abbey, *16*
  Bury St. Edmunds Abbey, *130, 131, 137*
  Byland Abbey, 63; *32*
  Canterbury Cathedral Abbey, *112; 127, 128*
  Chester Cathedral Abbey, *41, 94, 96, 99, 122*
  Crowland Abbey, *21*
  Dorchester Priory, *50*
  Durham Cathedral Abbey, *97, 100*
  Ely Cathedral Abbey, *121*
  Evesham Abbey, *11, 129*
  Ewenny Priory, *55*
  Glastonbury Abbey, *30, 110, 124*
  Gloucester Cathedral Abbey, *75*
  Lastingham Priory, *72*
  Lindisfarne Priory, *31*

INDEX

Benedictine foundations—(contd.)
  Malmesbury Abbey, *15, 35*
  Malvern Priory, *12*
  Milton Abbas, *8*
  Muchelney Abbey, *123*
  Norwich Cathedral Abbey, *101*
  Pershore Abbey, *44*
  Romsey Abbey, *40, 51*
  St. Alban's Abbey, *77, 79, 82, 83*
  St. Mary's Abbey, *23*
  Selby Abbey, *70*
  Sherborne Abbey, *1 , 49*
  Shrewsbury Abbey, *48, 109*
  Tewkesbury Abbey, *9, 34, 42*
  Tynemouth Priory, *88*
  Westminster Abbey, *52, 59, 60, 85*
  Whitby Abbey, 2; *17*
  Winchester Cathedral Abbey, *78, 84*
Benedictines, 91
Bernard, St., denunciation, 3
Birkenhead Priory, *93*
Bishops—
  relations with, 74
  visitations, 73
Black Canons, *see* Augustine, St., Order of
Blyth Abbey, *56*
Bolton Priory, 6
Bovarii, 96
Boxgrove Priory, *47*
Boys in Monasteries, 14, 26
Bridlington Priory, *53*
Bradford Abbas, *126*
Bridges, building, 101
Bruno, St., Order of, 4
Buckfast Abbey, *16*
Building costs, 85
Building methods, 79
Buildwas Abbey, *65*
Bury St. Edmunds Abbey, *75, 89, 105, 112*
Bursar, 66
Byland Abbey, *64; 31*

Calder Abbey, *33*
Canons—
  duties of, 28
  regular, 6
  secular, 6
Canterbury Cathedral Abbey, *102, 127, 128*
  fire in, 82
Carlisle Cathedral, 6
Carthusians, 4
Carthusian planning, 55
Cartmel Priory, *62*
Castle Acre Priory, *27, 119*
Cellarer, office of, 16
Censarii, 95
Ceremonial, 63
Chamberlain, office of, 20
Chapter and Chapter House, 44 f., 58 f.
Charterhouses, 4, 89; *57*
Chester Cathedral Abbey, 88; *41, 94, 96, 99, 122*
Christchurch Priory, *61*
Circator, office of, *57, 62*
Cistercian foundations—
  Abbey Dore, *39; 45, 46*
  Beaulieu Abbey, *46; 108*
  Buildwas Abbey, *65*
  Byland Abbey, *64; 32*
  Carlisle Cathedral, 6
  Cleeve Abbey, *106, 107*
  Fountains Abbey, *37, 39, 42, 51; 2, 7, 37, 71, 103, 111, 115, 116, 117*
  Furness Abbey, *69, 80*
  Holme Cultram, *39*
  Netley Abbey, *68*
  Newminster Abbey, *42; 87*
  Rievaulx Abbey, 4; *5, 20, 29, 104*
  Roche Abbey, *24, 138*
  Tintern Abbey, *3*
  Valle Crucis Abbey, *44, 95; 26*
  Whalley Abbey, *73*
Cistercian planning, 38
Cistercian refectory, 47
Cistercian regulations, 4
Cistercians, 91

Citeaux, Monastery of, 3
Claustral buildings, 52
Cleeve Abbey, *106*, *107*
Cloister, arrangement of, 43
Clothes, monks', 20
Cluniac Order foundations—
    Castle Acre Priory, *27*, *119*
    Much Wenlock, *120*
Cluniac Order, 2
Cluny, 2
Collation, 62
Conduct, 61
Convent, the, 10
Conversi, 31
Corrodies, 34
Cotsetti, 96
Craftsmen, employment of, 90, 93
Croxden Abbey, 14
Cruciform planning, 38

Daily Life, 56
Daniel, Walter, chronicler, 11
Diet, *see* Food
Dominican Order of Friars, 8
Dominican Nuns in Quire, *frontispiece*
Dorchester Priory, 50
Dorter, 45; *116*
Dover Priory, 12, 53, 102
Drainage, 88
Dunstable Abbey, 76
Dunstan, St., 2
Durham Cathedral Abbey, 97, *100*

Education, 26, 94
Election, dues on, 74
Ely Cathedral Abbey, *121*
Evesham Abbey, *11*, *129*
Ewenny Priory, 55
Expense of visitors, 73

Fairs, revenue from, 71
Farmery—
    plan, 52
    treatment in, 21
Farming, monastic, 95, 97

Finance, monastic, 66
Fisheries, 71
Flogging, 59
Food in monasteries, 17 f., 34, 48, 52, 58, 60
Fountains Abbey, 37, 39, 42, 51; *2*, *7*, *37*, *71*, *103*, *111*, *115*, *116*, *117*
Franciscan Friars, 8
Frater, 47
    conduct in, 61
Fraterer, office of, 19
Friars, Order of, 8
Furness Abbey, 69, 80

Gatehouses, 53
Gervase, 81, 83
Gilbert, St., 7
Gilbertines, 7, 27, 32; *118*
Glastonbury Abbey, 2, 5, 110; *5*, *30*, *124*
Gloucester Cathedral Abbey, 75, 89, 105, 112
Grainger, the, 27
Grey Friars, *see* Franciscan Friars
Grey Friars, Coventry, 86
Guesthouse, *see* Hospitality
Guisborough Priory, 22

Habits, *see* Clothes
Haughmond Abbey, 91, *113*, *125*
Henry III, 84
Hexham Priory, 39; *43*, *74*, *98*
Hierarchy, the monastic, 10
Hilda, St., 2
Hinton Charterhouse, 57
Holme Cultram, 39
Hospitality, 23, 68, 93
Hosteller, office of, 23

John of Gaunt's, Bristol, *see* St. Mark's Hospital

Kirkham, Gateway, 78
Kirkstead, Chapel at, 54
Kirkstall Abbey, *28*
Kitchens, 48

INDEX

Kitchener, office of, 18
Knights Hospitallers and Knights Templars, *see* Military Orders

Lacock, 7, 43; *90, 92*
Lady Chapels, 38
Lady Mass, 58
Lands, 32, 57
Landlords, monasteries as, 95
Lanercost Priory, *13*
Lastingham Priory, *72*
Lavatory, 20, 49, 50
Lay Brethren, *see* Conversi
Lay duties of abbeys, 101
Liber Albus of Worcester, 77; *67*
Libraries, monastic, 9, 14, 93
Lindisfarne Priory, *31*
Literature, 92
Llanthony Priory, 4, *64*

Malmesbury Abbey, *15, 35*
Malvern Priory, *12*
Masons, 80
Mastermason, 79 f., 85
Matins, 62
Meals, *see* Food
Meaux, 37
Melrose, 4
Menus, 60
Military Orders, 7, 8
Milton Abbas, *8*
Mission-work of friars, 9
Monasteries, mixed, 72
Monastic buildings, the, 37, 79
Monastic debts, 67
Monastic libraries, 93
Monastic relations, 102
Monastic revenues, 69
Monasticism, advent of, 1
Monks, duties of, 28
Mortmain, statute of, 99
Much Wenlock, 50; *120*
Muchelney Abbey, *123*

Necessarium, *see* Rere-dorter
Netley Abbey, 68

Newminster Abbey, 42; *87*
Nomination, methods of, 11
Nones, 61
Norrys, Abbot of Evesham, 12
Norton Priory, *38*; Lectern, 57
Norwich Cathedral Abbey, *101*
Novices, 29, 61
Nuns—
  Church at Romsey, 7; *1*
  in Gilbertine order, 7

Obedientiaries, 10, 65, 66
Observances, *see* Barnwell
Odo, Abbot of Cluny, 2
Office of Deed, illumination, *54*

Paris, Matthew, chronicler, 11, 79
Parishioners, disputes with, 41
Patronage, 70
Peasants Rising, The, 98
Pershore Abbey, 70; *44*
Pestilence, 77
Pontefract Priory, 102
Precentor, office of, 13
Premonstratensians, 6; *114*
Premontre, Abbey of, 6
Prior, office of, 12, 13
Prisons, monastic, 23
Processions, 59, 62–63

Quarries, 86, 87
Quire, monastic, enclosed, 39

Refectory (Fountains Abbey), *103, 104*
Regulations for monks, 28 f., 61, 62
Rere-dorter, 45; *115*
Rievaulx Abbey, 4; *5, 20, 29, 104*
Rioting, anti-monastic, 27, 98, 103
Roche Abbey, 24, *138*
Romsey Abbey, 7; *40, 51*

Sampson, Abbot, St. Edmundsbury, 16, 17, 67
Sanctuary Men, 36
St. Alban's Abbey, 77, 79, 82, *83*
St. Bartholomew's Priory, London, 66
St. Botolph's Priory, Colchester, 67

St. Edmundsbury, 15
St. Germains Priory, Cornwall, 19
St. Mark's Hospital, 81
St. Mary's Abbey, York, 23
St. Osyth's Abbey, 133
Sacrist, Office of, 15
Schools, monastic, 26, 54
Seising, 70
Selby Abbey, 70
Servants, Hired, 33, 94
Services, 56 ff., 96, 97
Servii, 41
Sherborne, 41
Sherborne Abbey, 10, 49
Shrewsbury Abbey, 48, 109
Sick, care of, see Farmery
Singing, monastic, 13 f.
Slype, 43
Social reactions, 91
Steward, see Bailiff
Stone, see Quarries
Strata Florida Abbey, 36
Succentor, 13
Sub-cellarer, office of, 17
Sub-prior, office of, 12
Sunday procession, 62, 63
Suppression, 104

Taxation, 73 f.
Templars, order of, 8
Temporalities, 71
Tenants, 95
Tewkesbury Abbey, 9, 34, 42

Thornton Abbey, 132
Tierce, 59
Tintern Abbey, 3
Torre Abbey, 114
Towns, connection with, 71, 100
Trading, 72
Tynemouth Priory, 23; 88

Urban monasteries, 100

Valle Crucis Abbey, 44; 26, 95
Vespers, 61
Villeins, 96

Walsingham Priory, 25
Waltham Abbey, 136
Water supplies, 88
Watton Priory, 118
Welbeck, 6
Wenchepe, Prior of Dover, 12, 16
Westminster Abbey, 52; 59, 60, 85
Whalley Abbey, 73
Whitby Abbey, 2; 17
White Canons, see Premonstratensians
William of Sens, 83
Winchester Cathedral Abbey, 78, 84
Woodspring Priory, 58
Wool staple, 72
Worksop Priory, 14, 135

York, St. Mary's Abbey, mortar, 18
Yorkshire, 87, see also Cistercian

www.ingramcontent.com/pod-product-compliance
Lightning Source LLC
Chambersburg PA
CBHW070736160426
43192CB00009B/1466